PRAISE FOR

Paul Freiberger's

When Can You Start?

Freiberger delivers a fun and informative read. You will get a job a lot sooner if you read this book. Perfect for new grads at the beginning of their careers, and powerful ammunition for the rest of us.

—Guy Kawasaki, Founding Partner, Garage Technology Ventures, and Former Chief Evangelist of Apple

Highly useful to anyone facing an important job interview, especially if they haven't been practicing for a while. Practical and well-researched, with extensive and realistic examples. This will stand the test of time.

—Marc Singer, Director, McKinsey & Company

No one knows the job search process better than Paul Freiberger. In *When Can You Start?*, he cuts through all the rigmarole to truly help the job seeker, and he captures what everyone needs to know in a positive way.

—Richard Moran, CEO, Accretive Solutions

This book is powerful and expertly researched. Packed with interview advice you need to get your next job. Learn the right way to network and do informational interviews, how to handle "ambush" interviews, what to do with your phone during an interview, the right and wrong answers to

"What are your weaknesses?", and how to negotiate salary. And who knew that, not unlike dating, it turns out there's some pretty good advice on when you should or shouldn't make a follow-up call after an interview and when you can send a thank-you note. A fun read, this book both tastes good and is good for you.

—Larry Kramer, President and Publisher, *USA Today*

The most exhaustive, best researched book about job interviewing, filled with insights and research.

—Jean-Louis Gassée, General Partner, Allegis Capital

This is an excellent guide to a pivotal event in the hiring process—the interview. Paul has delivered an effective and pragmatic guide that should be read by anyone preparing for an interview.

—Avery Lyford, Chairman, the Churchill Club

A morale-boosting, inspiring book for your job search. You'll find solid, in-depth information for improving job interview skills crucial for success during your career, allowing you to soar during the most nerve-racking situations. Reading this book before your job search and interviews is like arming yourself before battle. Indispensable and empowering. There are many other books on job interviewing, but none have the combination of depth, techniques, tips, and tools that Freiberger provides in delightfully entertaining prose.

—Larry Jacobson, Motivational Speaker and Award-winning Author of *The Boy Behind the Gate*

Noted technologist Alan Kay said, "Perspective is worth 80 IQ points." Freiberger brings just such perspective with this fresh, highly engaging book. Ranging from millennia past to the latest in social media, the text draws from Freiberger's experiences as celebrated Silicon Valley historian, journalist, researcher, and consultant to large companies and individuals alike. Whether the reader is 18, 38, or 58, you will finish all the wiser from Freiberger's counsel.

—Brygg Ullmer, Associate Professor, LSU

I've seen a lot of career advice books in my three decades as corporate recruiter and career coach, but none of them were such fun to read. *When Can You Start?* is chock-a-block with great tips weaved into a narrative that is engaging and enlightening. Freiberger covers everything a job seeker needs to know to be a successful job candidate in clear, shimmering prose. He demystifies the interview process and reveals the thinking behind newer interview techniques, such as the so-called Google-type interview, that have unnerved job seekers recently. If you're looking to successfully navigate today's competitive job market, you need this book.

—Tom Ballantyne, Chief Career
Catalyst at Paths & Bridges

There are gems of wisdom packed into the sections on how to answer behavioral interview questions, how to succeed in a panel interview, and how to anticipate sensitive and challenging questions. The principles and practices discussed in this book will help the job seeker turn the interview from an interrogation into a conversation.

—Marcia G. Rhodes, WorldatWork,
Director of Public Relations

Informative and insightful, Paul Freiberger's *When Can You Start?* is an essential resource for any job seeker.

—Lisa Thompson, Human Resources Executive,
Mammoth Mountain Ski Area

WHEN
CAN YOU
START?

WHEN
CAN YOU
START?

ACE the
Job Interview
and GET HIRED

PAUL FREIBERGER

When Can You Start?
By Paul Freiberger

Career Upshift Productions
801 E. 16th Ave.
San Mateo, CA 94402

Publisher's Cataloging-In-Publication Data
(Prepared by The Donohue Group, Inc.)

Freiberger, Paul, 1953-
   When can you start? : ace the job interview and get hired /
Paul Freiberger.

   p. ; cm.

   Includes bibliographical references and index.
   Issued also as an ebook.
   ISBN: 978-0-9887028-0-6

   1. Employment interviewing. 2. Job hunting. I. Title.

HF5549.5.I6 F74 2013
650.14/4

PB ISBN: 978-0-9887028-0-6
eBook ISBN: 978-0-9887028-1-3

Printed in the United States of America

Book and Cover Design: 1106 Design

For Jeanne

Contents

Introduction   xiii

1. Preparation: An Oxygen Tank for the
Job Interviewee   1

2. Design Your Research Manual   7

3. Master the Informational Interview   19

4. New Rules for the Phone Interview   35

5. The Only Question You Must Be Able
to Answer   49

6. (Don't) Tell Me About Your Weaknesses   63

7. How to Succeed in a Panel Interview   83

8. Where Does the Law Draw the Line?   97

9. Trick Questions   111

10. Say "Thank You" and Mean It   123

11. The New Interview, Courtesy of Google
and Others   131

12. Turn the Tables: When It's Your Turn to
    Pose Questions   149

13. A Guide to Salary Negotiation   167

14. More Linchpins for Success   187

15. The Ideal Interview   203

References   217

Acknowledgments   219

Index   223

Introduction

I was 16 when I had my very first job interview. I wanted to earn enough money to pay for a driver-education class—an early example of the great importance of employment and the job interview.

My dad drove me to the meeting, all the while offering sample interview questions I could expect and advice about how to make a good impression.

Entering the workplace, I was nervous as I introduced myself to the manager. But I worked hard to focus. I wanted that job so badly.

Thanks to the preparation and some beginner's luck, I handled all the questions, including those about my work ethic, punctuality, and customer service techniques. I still remember the moment when the manager turned to me and uttered those four delightful words: "When can you start?"

I started that day as a cook at Jack in the Box in Mineola, New York. I felt so lucky to get the job. It was a feeling that I would have throughout my career each time someone offered me a position. From that day forward, I made it a point to become an expert on job interviewing.

In addition to working as a cook, I interviewed and was hired for summer jobs during my high school and college years as a janitor, a construction worker, and a bookstore stock boy.

Over the years, I had dozens of job interviews, including informational interviews, phone screening interviews, panel interviews, written questionnaires, and one-on-one interviews. I had my share of miserable interviews and embarrassing moments. There were times I could tell my lack of enthusiasm was evident, or I had simply answered a question in a way that had managed to get me eliminated. I've experienced the frustration every job applicant has felt.

But through it all, I have generally stayed employed— proof positive that the right interview preparation brings opportunity. Like so many of us in our fast-paced global economy, I've moved through several careers. I've been a successful magazine editor, newspaper reporter, project manager, corporate communications strategist, and small business owner.

After a career as a journalist and award-winning author writing about technology, I decided I wanted to work in the area of technology research. I applied for a job recruiting, hiring, and managing teams at a research laboratory. To make that career shift, I had an all-day panel interview and several one-on-one interviews.

Fast forward nine years when I began another career change, applying for a position at the global management consulting firm McKinsey & Company. McKinsey is a prestigious place to work, but it's also famous for its grueling job interviews. *Forbes* reports that it has the toughest interview process, bar none.

The first thing I did when I decided to interview at McKinsey was to buy a new suit. What better excuse to fix my wardrobe? Fortunately, I also prepared, writing out answers for likely questions and practicing them over and over. Preparing for the McKinsey interview won me the job of corporate communications director. Just as important, it also gave me many new insights into the job-search process and laid the groundwork for this book.

During my time at McKinsey, colleagues and friends increasingly began calling on me for advice about how to advance in their careers. They had seen how well interview preparation had worked for me, and they wanted to know my secret.

That was how I discovered the satisfaction in sharing what I have learned and giving other people the tools to ace the interview and win the job. I now run a successful business called Shimmering Resumes that has helped thousands of job seekers craft the ideal resume, prepare for job interviews, and set their career on a whole new trajectory.

In *When Can You Start?*, I share with you much of what I've learned about how to succeed at job interviews. From jobs cooking burgers and washing dishes to positions reporting on business (*InfoWorld*, the *San Francisco Examiner*, and the *San Jose Mercury News*), managing technology R & D (Interval Research), and overseeing communications strategy at a celebrated global company (McKinsey & Company), I have enjoyed the challenges of career transition. I have seen the value and rewards of job interview preparation. This book is the distillation of the years of experience and insights I have gained.

It equips you with the knowledge and the tools to help avoid interview mistakes, be ready for the only interview question you must prepare to answer, ask the right questions in return, and negotiate the salary you deserve. You will learn how to turn things to your advantage in any interview, remain poised in what can be a highly stressful situation, and set yourself apart from the other candidates.

With the right preparation, even in the toughest of job markets, you *can* walk into the interview with a real advantage over the competition. Let's get started and see how it's done.

CHAPTER 1

Preparation: An Oxygen Tank for the Job Interviewee

All things are ready, if our mind be so.
—William Shakespeare, *Henry V*

An out-of-towner with concert tickets is lost in New York City. A man on the corner is playing violin for passersby. The out-of-towner approaches. "How do you get to Carnegie Hall?" he asks. The reply: "Practice, practice, practice."

A joke as old as this one earns its longevity, at least in part, by containing a grain of truth: as a general rule, a performance becomes worthy of the highest acclaim only if it has been preceded by a great deal of preparation.

Preparation is especially important in two situations: when the performer rarely performs and when there is a lot at stake.

You're not a professional musician, though, so how does all this apply to you?

Your Turn in the Spotlight

From time to time, most of us find ourselves in a situation that is the very definition of a performance. It's a performance we don't do very often, and we usually have a lot riding on the outcome.

That performance is the job interview.

The interview is the last step in a long and important process, and it can be a make-or-break moment with the potential to change your life. Is there any doubt that, for this performance, you want to be as ready as you've ever been?

It would take a special kind of indifference or insanity—or independent wealth—to approach an interview unprepared and merely hoping for the best, especially when the basics of preparation are so simple. There are two parts to job interview preparation: doing your homework and rehearsing.

Do Your Homework

If you had just been cast as Hamlet, you'd want to know something about the play. You'd want to know what the playwright was getting at with all that archaic language, so your lines would roll trippingly off the tongue.

If you were hired to appear with the New York Philharmonic as the featured player in a Mozart piano concerto, you'd want to know what the orchestra would be doing behind you while you were out there banging on the keys.

If you were about to interview with a company, you'd want to know as much about that company as possible. You'd want to know its history. How is it structured? What are its strengths? What challenges does it face? What's the latest industry news? What do you bring to the table for this company, in this industry and at this time?

It's all a matter of preparation. The answers to those questions do not come out of the blue. They come from research that must be done in advance of any interview.

Anticipate questions the employer will ask, and develop answers. This is simply essential. Put yourself in the interviewer's place and formulate questions based on the three issues employers most want addressed:

Can you do the work?

Your resume will largely answer this question, which involves your experience in similar positions, your education, and your other skills. But the interview will let the employer sense your capacities in a direct, personal way, and it can make the deepest impression. For instance, studies show that we think confident people are competent—more competent than they statistically are.

Will we enjoy working with you?

You can have all the ability in the world and fail on fit. Fit—and more broadly, interpersonal skills—relates to competence, since if you can't get along with the boss, the board, your peers, and your staff, you will have problems doing the job. The interview exists above all to answer questions on fit, personality, and character. Note that the more you know about the company, the more you already fit in.

How much do you want to succeed in the job?

An oft-repeated myth holds that employers care how much you want the job. If you're desperate for it, interviewers will be less likely to hire you. In fact, companies really want to know how much you want *job success*—that is, how vigorously you will perform. (Of course, if they sense you're not interested in the job, they will conclude you're not interested in success either.)

Investor Warren Buffett hires on three main criteria—ability, character, and energy—and this drive for job success equates to the third one. You can show your commitment to success by your preparation. How much do you already know about the company? If you know a lot, employers will deduce that you will aggressively learn about other companies, customers, and techniques for improvement.

Rehearsal Time

There may be some gifted improvisers out there who don't need to rehearse—but, for the vast majority of us, a job interview is an alien situation in which we're not immediately comfortable.

You want to be perceived as bright, enthusiastic, knowledgeable, and articulate. You may even *be* bright, enthusiastic, knowledgeable, and articulate, but those qualities may not always bubble to the surface in a high-pressure encounter. There are simple steps you can take to give yourself the best shot, and we'll cover them in the following chapters of this book:

- Learn about the kinds of questions interviewers are known to ask.

- Compile a list of those questions, with representative examples of each type: traditional questions, behavioral questions, puzzle questions, and odd questions.

- Be sure to take a hard look at your resume, find the weak points, and focus some questions on those points.

- Think through your answers.

- Think through your own questions. One of the most important interview moments occurs when the interviewer asks if you have any questions of your own.

- Enlist someone to conduct a mock interview with you, but don't just read from a script. Let that person select questions from your list.

- If you don't have someone to rehearse with, invest in professional coaching.

- Get feedback.

- If you can, videotape your mock interview. Seeing yourself through the all-too-objective lens of the camera can be an eye-opening moment.

- Practice.

- Practice.

- Practice.

The good news is that improvements typically happen very quickly. At that point, Carnegie Hall should be just around the corner.

CHAPTER 2

Design Your Research Manual

If you torture the data long enough,
Nature will confess.

—Ronald Coase, Winner of the Nobel Prize in Economics

One of the most important things to do in the early stages of finding a job is research. Even if you have been in your industry for upwards of 20 years and have tons of hands-on experience, it is essential that you put in the time to make sure you have the most current information at your fingertips.

Knowing the companies that are worth applying to, the topics to highlight during the job screening process, and the names to drop during an interview to completely bowl over the hiring manager is not going to happen by sheer luck. You need to arm yourself by doing systematic and targeted research.

The more information you have collected about your industry and the ins and outs of the culture at your potential new company, the more confident you will sound. Proper preparation will keep the right answers on the tip of your tongue rather than way back in the deep recesses of distant memory.

That you are able to respond quickly with current information will impress a hiring manager far more than any resume ever could. You need to be able to leap off the page and not simply rest your chances on what you've written there.

Get Schooled in Your Field

Maybe you went to college to get the training and education required for your chosen career path. Maybe you already have your foot in the door and have a basic on-the-job understanding of how your chosen industry works.

Either way, the devil is in the details. If the future of an industry appears to be on a severe downswing, it might be time to try and take your skill set in a different direction.

In order to learn whether a career has growth potential or is dying a slow death, you can visit the Bureau of Labor Statistics' official website (www.bls.gov). There, you can access the government's expected job growth projections for the next few years in your chosen field.

There's no use putting tons of effort into getting a particular job today if it is likely the position might well not exist two or three years down the line.

Brush Up Your Skill Set

If the outlook does look bright for the job you're eyeballing, your next step is to make sure you meet all of the latest requirements it will take for you to merit consideration for the position.

You may need to do some training, such as a short-term certificate program or workshop. These career courses may be offered through a local university extension program, online, or by civic job training organizations.

Sometimes a degree is not enough. For example, if you are going into the computer science industry, you may want to get a variety of Microsoft certificates to prove that you know about networking and other must-have skills in advance of your job interview. It could be terribly embarrassing to get in front of a hiring manager only to be told you lack prerequisites that you could have easily obtained prior to your meeting.

What Counts as an Interview?

Today, the job interview is an utterly standard part of every job application, surpassing even the resume in its universality. A resume is almost always part of the job-seeking process, but the word *almost* is there for a reason: for some jobs, applicants are asked to fill out a form application instead of submitting a resume. However, even when you don't need a resume, employers insist on having a few words with you before they sign you up. The conversation might not take place in person, but words will be exchanged before you end up on the payroll.

Was it always thus? If not, how did it begin? When did people start interviewing other people? If interviews were once rare, how did they become ubiquitous?

To answer those questions, we need to have a clear idea of what we are really asking. What is a job? What counts as an interview?

As to the first question, it's best to keep things simple. A job is an activity that you do for someone else for pay. Payment does not have to be monetary. It can be almost anything of value, including room and board.

Does that value have to be concrete? For our purposes, it can be relatively abstract. Internships are typically unpaid, but interns are rewarded with experience, or the chance to make contacts or burnish their resumes. Internships these days look like jobs in almost every respect other than the receipt of a paycheck.

To qualify as a job, a position cannot be gained via heredity. If your expectation is to take over the family farm from your father, and you accede to the position automatically, that's something different. You may work harder than the hired hand, but he is the one with a job.

As to the second question, an interview is a communication between an applicant and an employer or the employer's agent. It can be written. An interview can be an exchange of letters or emails, or an online chat. It does not have to occur in person. A phone call or an online videoconference can be an interview.

Read All About It!

You can never be too informed on the latest trends and industry buzz in a field in which you are interested in working. After all, what better way is there to prove to a prospective employer that you are truly passionate about an industry than by being completely up-to-date on its most important developments?

To learn about the latest trends, utilize any, or all, of the following online magazines and websites:

Computer science: *MIT news*
(http://web.mit.edu/newsoffice/topic/
computers.html)

Education: *Education News*
(www.educationnews.org)

Engineering and science: *ScienceDaily*
(www.sciencedaily.com)

Health: *ModernHealthcare.com*
(www.modernhealthcare.com)

Hospitality: *Hospitality Net*
(www.hospitalitynet.org/list/11-20/
154000430.html)

Management: *Bloomberg Businessweek*
(www.businessweek.com)

Human Resources: *WorldatWork*
(www.worldatwork.org)

Other sources of information about trends include:

- Books

- Twitter and other social media sites

- LinkedIn and other networking sites

You should also make every effort to become fluent in the lingo or jargon particular to your chosen field. Every industry has its own unique vocabulary, and hiring managers take it for granted that potential employees will understand it.

If an interviewer uses an acronym instead of the actual term for something, you need to know what that acronym means. There are websites devoted to helping people learn some of the more common terminology associated with certain industries. The following list is just a sample.

Automotive: Specialty Equipment Market Association (www.sema.org/acronyms)

Computer science: IPC (www.ipc.org/ContentPage.aspx?pageid= Industry-Acronyms)

Healthcare and medicine: Health IT (http://healthit.hhs.gov/portal/server.pt/ community/health_it_hhs_gov__acronyms/1217)

Hospitality: Technomic (www.technomic.com/Resources/Industry_Facts/ dyn_acronyms.php)

Remember, the more you know about your industry, the easier the entire job-search process will be for you. Crafting a targeted resume, deciding which company to seek out first, and fielding questions during the interview or screening process are going to be so much simpler when you are armed with the latest knowledge.

By doing the research, you can avoid any dead ends in the application process before you've wasted too much of your precious job-search time.

If the task of researching seems too overwhelming to you, or you're not sure exactly where to begin, a good starting point is to look at the business guides on the website of the U.S. Small Business Administration (www.sba.gov/category/navigation-structure/starting-managing-business/managing-business/business-guides-industry). These guides can narrow your focus and get you headed down the right road for your particular field.

Put Yourself in Good Company

Once you've made sure that your chosen industry is the right place to conduct your job search, it's time to figure out which company's door to knock upon. In order to make the right call, you need to learn as much as possible about each potential employer.

In the category of "things you need to know," you'll find the following key questions, to which you should have all the answers before sending out your resume:

- How big is the company?

- What is the firm's growth potential?

- Has there been any recent news regarding the company?

- What is the culture of the company like?

- What kind of management style has this firm adopted?

- Are there any policies particular to this corporation?

- How is this business perceived by the public at large, as well as by its peers?

- How profitable is this company?

When you take the time to do the research on companies before you apply to them, you can ensure you won't be blindsided by anything that might be included in a job offer down the line.

Sometimes, your research may uncover that, in order to work for one of the better companies within an industry, you will need to relocate. If that doesn't fit into your plans, then be sure to focus your attention solely on companies that are geographically tolerable to your current situation.

That a firm has a lot of name prestige is not enough reason for you to waste your time as well as theirs if you don't have any real intention of working for them. You may think it's a good thing to be able to say you turned down a job offer from a Fortune 500 company, but while that provides you with a temporary ego boost, it really doesn't get you any closer to long-term employment.

Here are websites where you can get the answers to some of the questions on your list:

- The Business Journals (www.bizjournals.com) is a great website for finding information on small and mid-sized companies. Just type the name of a business you want to know about in the search box, and a list of all of the latest news will appear instantly before your eyes.

- Yahoo! Finance (http://finance.yahoo.com) can help you find various details about many publicly traded companies. If a company's stock prices are steadily headed downhill, it might be a red flag for job security going forward.

- All companies, both domestic and foreign, that operate in the United States must file various reports with the U.S. Securities and Exchange Commission. These can be found at the commission's site known as EDGAR (www.sec.gov/edgar.shtml). The information there can tell you how long a company has been in business and what licenses they hold.

- The Public Register (www.prars.com/index.php) is a storehouse for online annual reports for many companies. From an annual report, you can learn about the size of a company, see its profit and loss statements, and find out news that could impact the future of its financial well-being.

- The Riley Guide (www.rileyguide.com/research.html) provides comparisons of companies' financial information, ranking firms according to fiscal criteria to help you winnow out the pretenders from the contenders in your job search.

Go Straight to the Source

Of course, the best way to learn about a company is to get information straight from the horse's mouth. Visiting a company's website and reading how it describes itself can teach you tons about its philosophy and goals for the future. The site may also have a page specifically for prospective job applicants, detailing open positions and giving instructions on how and when to apply.

During a job interview, using some of the terminology and buzzwords from the company's own website is sure to signal to the interviewer that you've done your homework. It will place you in a favorable light.

Keep in mind, however, that no company is going to air its dirty laundry on its own corporate website. You should always be sure to verify the claims a company makes with a reliable independent source. One site that can speak to the financial strength of a company is A.M. Best (www.ambest.com/ratings/guide.asp).

Another extremely useful place to investigate is the Better Business Bureau (www.bbb.org/us/consumers), which can alert you to companies that have been flagged for being scams. If a business opportunity seems too good to be true, chances are it is, and the BBB will likely know about it.

Knowledge is Power

Once you've learned as much as you can about a prospective employer, you may discover that there are still questions to which you don't have the answers. That's perfectly fine. You should take a list of them with you to your job interview.

After you've given educated responses to all of the questions thrown your way, you'll likely be given a chance to ask some questions of your own. By being ready for this opportunity and asking relevant, company-specific questions, you can further prove yourself to be aware of what the most current topics of discussion happen to be.

Your research needs to be constant. The fact that you saw some news last month doesn't mean you're fully prepared, because the state of affairs is always in flux. When you're getting ready to submit another round of resumes, make sure you do your due diligence to make sure that nothing has changed dramatically in the interim.

Remember, before you even pick up the phone to find out who is hiring, you need to do your research. Take notes, print out important articles, and form opinions based upon the various topics being discussed within your industry. These will prove invaluable throughout your job search and job interviews, and will reward you heavily.

If it sounds like a lot of work, it is. But hard work pays off. If you're serious about finding a job that will last for many years to come, you owe it to yourself to start working now.

CHAPTER 3

Master the Informational Interview

*The time to repair the roof is
when the sun is shining.*
—John F. Kennedy

A long with crafting the killer resume and putting together the best possible cover letter, research and networking are the cornerstones of a serious job search.

Research matters because it guides your search. You learn the landscape because that helps you to perfect your resume and cover letter. When you get to the next phase, you hone your interview strategy to reflect what your research has taught you. Research allows you to focus. It lets you leave the generic behind so you can present yourself as the specific answer to the needs of a specific employer.

Networking matters because it can introduce you to openings you might have missed and because it supplements your research with a more personal picture of a company or an industry.

In many ways, research and networking have overlapping purposes. They complement each other. One underused strategy takes advantage of that overlap and should be part of every applicant's arsenal: the informational interview.

Despite its value, the informational interview has become the poor relation in the family of career strategies. It gets little attention in job-hunting guides, but it should be a standard tactic for job seekers. If anything, the fact that it is so often forgotten makes it more valuable to those who take the trouble to do something a little different.

The informational interview can best be introduced by describing what it is not. First, it is emphatically not a job interview. You are not responding to a job posting or a recruiter's call. Second, it is not the exclusive province of job hunters. Anyone, employed or not, can benefit. Third, you are not being interviewed. The roles are reversed, and you are the one asking the questions.

An informational interview takes place between a professional employed in a particular field and an individual who is either considering a similar career or is already working in that same field or a related industry. In a job interview, you often know little, if anything, about the person across the table. It may be someone from the company's human resources staff, an interviewer who has some definite notions of proper interview subjects but little or no direct experience of the job opening in question.

That person would be a good choice as the subject for an informational interview if your goal is a career in HR. If your goal lies elsewhere, the best person to choose is someone with hands-on, day-to-day experience in your field of interest, someone who knows the job from the inside, even if she has not the slightest notion of hiring procedures or staff recruitment.

The Benefits of Informational Interviews

With that kind of interview subject, a student or new graduate, or anyone seriously considering a career change, has the chance to develop a broader and more accurate concept of the reality of working within a specific job or industry. Once you learn some of the realities of a particular trade or position, you have useful information that will help you make a realistic decision about whether this work is a good fit for you.

This can be especially beneficial if you have only an academic perspective on the field, a common handicap. Ask a lawyer, for example, about the difference between law school and actual practice. School is a world of almost philosophical analysis of judicial decisions; practice is often a mundane exercise in the routine of real estate closings and corporate bookkeeping.

In the worst case, an informational interview might teach you that your picture of the work bears little resemblance to reality. That can be a profoundly deflating bit of knowledge, but it is almost always better to have your illusions shattered early on, when you still have the opportunity to regroup and consider a different career path.

Beyond acquiring detailed industry, company, and career information from actual employers and employees, another benefit of these meetings is the potential they provide you to make new industry-specific contacts to add to your network. Whether you are looking for an entry-level job or an executive position, informational interviews can expand your professional network and play a vital role in helping you discover the hidden job market. According to Cornell University Career Services, up to 80 percent of all job openings are not advertised; rather, they are filled through networking and professional contacts. Informational interviews and any networking that stems from them are excellent ways to gain access to this fruitful hidden job market.

Seeking Out Informational Interview Opportunities

Preparation is essential to the success of informational interviewing. Although it may have the sound of an old homily, this is a piece of advice that cannot be safely ignored. The first and most obvious step is to have a clear idea of the career or careers that interest you the most. Once you have narrowed the field, excellent places to start your search for potential interview candidates are professional associations, current business contacts, friends, teachers, and online job networking groups.

If you are just starting out, your resource list may be short and not especially helpful, but don't be discouraged. That list will likely expand once you participate in an informational interview or two. A general search for companies within the industry, local Rotary Clubs, online networking systems, and alumni groups can help get the ball rolling if you have limited contacts within your field of interest.

Using the Internet

Many of those resources have been around for a while, and Abraham Lincoln could have availed himself of similar ones when considering his career; but access to the connected world of the Web vastly increases your reach. Facebook, for all its ubiquity, is not necessarily the place to start. It's a social network above all else, and using it to make this kind of connection is almost guaranteed to undercut the seriousness and sincerity of any overture you make. This is not Facebook's forte.

A better option is a website with a more professional orientation, and the obvious choice is LinkedIn. The site makes no secret of its role as "the world's largest professional network" or of its focus on career development.

It is a natural place to look for industry connections. Before you start that search, take some time to make the most of your LinkedIn profile. When you contact someone through the site, your profile is the first place they'll look. You can, of course, attach a copy of your resume to any messages you send, but it's preferable to let contacts ask for it in their own time. Bombarding contacts with resumes is not the way to win their hearts and minds, and you can be certain they'll check your profile in any event. Make sure it's ready.

LinkedIn does not treat all your contacts the same. You can easily message people with whom you are directly connected, called 1st-degree connections in the LinkedIn taxonomy. People who are connected to those connections are your 2nd-degree connections, and you can invite them to connect. Your 3rd-degree connections are connected to that 2nd-degree group, and the availability of opportunities for you to invite them to connect varies. More distant connections can still be approached via in-site messaging, but you cannot always issue a direct invitation.

The bottom line is that not everyone is instantly available for you to contact, but there are two options that can help. First, LinkedIn provides a system of groups that its members can join, including industry-specific, corporate, alumni, and trade groups. Members of any group you join automatically become part of your LinkedIn network. Second, there are options outside the LinkedIn system. It is often possible to track down the email addresses of the people you wish to contact, and you can write to them directly. Admittedly, the recipient of an unsolicited email may not always respond favorably, so this approach needs careful handling.

People sometimes hesitate to contact the most likely interview subjects. Those subjects are, after all, busy and successful, hardly the types to have abundant spare time for something as frivolous as an informational interview.

In reality, however, you may find a surprisingly sympathetic audience. That sympathy may not be universal; but, like the old advice about cocktail party chit-chat, you are asking people to do something they love: Talk about themselves. Many of them have been in your position early in their careers. They understand why you're there; and, being human, they're flattered by your interest. People enjoy the role of helpful adviser.

To nurture those positive feelings, plan your approaches to your potential subjects with care.

How to Land an Informational Interview

First, prepare. Take plenty of time to research companies or potential interviewees on your list. Learn about their job descriptions and relevant business ventures. If the industry is completely new to you, be prepared to learn some of the terminology and job specifics before making any interview requests. Going into an informational interview with a bit of insight shows motivation, enthusiasm, and genuine interest. This pre-interview homework can pay off in the long run, particularly if you harbor hopes of learning about any hidden job opportunities.

Even if you think you have a red-hot lead, be patient. It makes no sense to rush the process. Do your homework first, and wait until you have enough time to manage the interview comfortably. Don't squeeze it into an overbooked schedule.

Get in touch with your resources or contact the companies that provide services in your career field. How you ask for an informational interview will depend on factors such as location, type of business, and the person's position and hours of availability. The most common approaches are in person, via email, by standard post, and by telephone.

Some principles apply regardless of the medium you choose. Be brief. Be clear—especially clear that this is not a hiring appeal. Be polite and appreciative. Say something about yourself and something about your reason for selecting this particular person; your research should have prepared you for this. Be ready for rejection, and be equally ready to accept that rejection gracefully. This is not the time to persist in the face of your contact's evident lack of interest.

If making the request in writing, carefully formulate the text and specifically state your purpose. Phone attempts may require you to handle gatekeepers before you actually reach the decision maker, so have a similar script for them prepared when you call. It may take several calls before your request is acknowledged, and this is where persistence can pay off. However, use caution not to be overbearing in your efforts and, again, be willing to take "no" for an answer.

If an interview is forthcoming, let your contact set the terms. This is a favor, not an obligation, so time, place, and method are not your decisions. Some contacts will be happy to see you in person. Others will offer some time on the phone. Either method is perfectly viable.

Developing a List of Interview Questions

Since you have already done some of the basic research, you should now hone in on the specifics. Find out more about your interviewee and, especially, about the latest developments in the field. If you do that, you will be able to ask questions that are more meaningful and more personalized, and asking good questions is one more way to demonstrate your genuine interest and your relevant knowledge.

You will want to compile a list of questions beforehand that cover those aspects of the work that are most important to you. Keep your questions open-ended. Questions that can be answered with a simple "yes" or "no" are dead ends. In order for you to gain any insight from the experience, the interview must expand into a working conversation between two people with shared interests. Open-ended questions push things in that direction.

Ask not only about job specifics but also about the profession and industry in general, your contact's career path, and the day-to-day lifestyle impact of the job. Ask about educational requirements, not only in the field today but in the past and in the future. What changes have there been? Where are things headed? What's different today? By understanding the development of a field and its requirements, you can assess your own qualifications, plan how to get prepared, and prioritize key items on your resume.

Consider using some of these questions as starting points:

- What is the outlook for this industry or profession? What changes have you seen over the course of your career?

- What specialized education or training is required? How has that changed?

- What skills or talents have you found most useful? How has that changed? How do you see that changing in the future?

- Are there possibilities for advancement within this position? What qualities have been most important in that respect?

- Can you describe your average workday and your key job responsibilities?

- What are the best and worst things about this position today?

- Is there a team effort or approach to your work?

- What resources help you keep up with the field? What trade or professional associations have you found useful? What would you recommend?

- What has surprised you over the course of your career? What changes have you found most challenging?

- What are the average starting salary and pay range for this type of work?

- Is there room for individuality in this position, or are there strict protocols to follow?

- Describe the work environment here—is it relaxed, exciting, or competitive?

- How did you enter the field, and what jobs have you held within it?

- Would you do it again? What would you do differently?

- What is the industry career path like today?

- What industry or technological changes are influencing this field currently?

- How flexible are the work schedule, job location, dress code, and vacation time?

- In what ways does this job affect your life outside of work? How have you been able to maintain an acceptable work/life balance? How do you see work/life balance issues affecting colleagues?

Aside from questions that are ridiculously inappropriate ("How did you rate such a hot assistant?"), there is only one absolute taboo: Don't ask for a job. That's not why you are here. When you asked for the interview, you entered into a sort of contract as to its terms. Keep your side of the bargain and you'll stay on friendly terms with your contact. If you break your promise, that is not likely to be forgotten.

On the other hand, do not hesitate to ask about things that are specific to your employment situation. It's fair game to ask how your existing skills and education fit into the field and how you can improve your prospects in the future.

The Day of the Informational Interview

Prepare by reviewing your notes and questions the day before the interview, and plan what you will wear. Dress professionally to make a good first impression.

Make a last-minute check of industry news. If something big has happened in the past few days, you want to be able to discuss it, and it can be a source of interview questions that touch on subjects that may already be on your contact's mind.

Bring along your list of questions, note-taking materials, and your resume or portfolio. You are not going to thrust your resume into your contact's hand, but you want to have it available if asked for it.

Ideally, show up at least 10 minutes early to the meeting, which will allow you time to take in the atmosphere and gather your thoughts. Take note of the names and positions of anyone you encounter, both before and after the meeting. If possible, get their business cards. These people might include assistants and receptionists. Remember that they are often gatekeepers and you may need their aid in the future.

Interview Procedures

When you finally meet your interviewee, open up the conversation in much the same way you would when meeting any professional contact or applying for a job. Introduce yourself, shake hands, be polite, show genuine interest, and thank the person for taking the time to see you. Before getting into your questions, request permission to take notes or record your conversation. The contact's answers are likely to bring up angles you had not considered previously, so new questions that are not on the list may work themselves into the conversation. Remember that this is not a job interview and there is nothing wrong with a conversation that ranges far afield.

During the encounter, keep an eye on the time. Unless the contact indicates a willingness to spend additional time with you, stick to the allotted period. If the limit is approaching, bring that up. That kind of awareness is a nice way to demonstrate your respect for the interviewee's time and his willingness to spend some of it on you. Don't hesitate to personalize the request: "If you were in my shoes, what would you do?"

Before the meeting wraps up, ask the contact for any recommendations concerning your goals. You can also ask if there are other contacts within the industry who might be willing to participate in an informational interview.

Thank your contact again, ask for a business card, and find out if it is acceptable for you to make contact in the future for industry-related purposes.

Following Through After the Meeting

Post-interview etiquette is extremely important and, properly managed, can lead to good things.

The first order of business is to send a thank-you note within 48 hours of the interview. Send a note to anyone you dealt with, not just the interviewee. Notes may be written by hand and personalized. Mention something specific about the interview. Keep things formal and professional.

If you're tempted to email your thanks, resist. Email, despite its many uses, is not ideal here.

Be sure to express your gratitude for the information your contact shared, and acknowledge any contacts he provided. If a contact gave you any remarkably insightful tips, make mention of those. Even if your contact was short on insight, mention something specific he said during your interview. Show that you were paying attention and valued the experience.

Your thank-you note does not have to be your last communication. One strategy that may help you tap into a company's hidden job market is to offer an occasional update. Let the interviewee know if you have made any progress within the industry because of the things you discussed in the interview. If you contact someone whose name your interviewee provided, you can legitimately use that as a reason for future communication. This keeps you on your contact's mind. You may even get a response that mentions some job openings.

On your own time, work up a summary of the interview from your notes. In particular, make note of the contacts you met or the names you were given. Decide whether to contact any of them for another round of informational interviews. After all, one interview is not likely to be enough to cement a career decision, and one person's experience may not be universal. Holding several of these brief meetings will expand your knowledge base while increasing your network of contacts, and those things matter.

The Long-Term Rewards

The informational interview is the best kind of rehearsal for actual job interviews. The situation is much the same, and you have the opportunity to practice your presentation in a setting that cannot be duplicated elsewhere.

You become more confident and you gain knowledge of your field from the inside. That combination is exactly the recipe that will make you stand out in future interactions with potential employers.

Up to 85 percent of job seekers secure their positions through networking, and the informational interview is, at the very least, a networking opportunity. That kind of opportunity can take you a long way in today's job market. Few job seekers can afford to ignore such an effective tool.

New Rules for the Phone Interview

We don't know where our first impressions come from or precisely what they mean, so we don't always appreciate their fragility.

—Malcolm Gladwell, *Blink*

When the job market gets tough, employers look for ways to weed out as many applicants as possible with the least possible expenditure of time and effort. In most fields, they have the luxury of choosing from an applicant pool whose numbers far outstrip the number of positions they wish to fill. While the employers' approach is certainly understandable, no one can blame job seekers for feeling that the market gets more difficult with each new development.

One such development that may take applicants by surprise is the ascendancy of the phone interview. In the recent past, a phone interview was a formality. It meant your paperwork had passed the first round of evaluation and you were likely to move on to the "real" interview as long as you could carry on a normal conversation with another human being. It was a chance to schedule an in-person interview, and that was when the real test would come. The phone interview was more of an administrative detail than a substantive challenge.

Today, however, times have changed. The phone interview can be a preliminary, or it can constitute a meaningful hurdle in the application process. Even the screening interview has become yet another part of the job seeker's burden that must be carefully managed. Start putting your house in order well in advance, with an understanding of the process, and some effective and practical preparation.

The Varieties of Phone Interviews

The screening interview

For many years, screening was the phone interview's sole purpose, and that purpose is still very much in play. In a screening interview, you are not speaking to someone who can hire you. You are not necessarily speaking to someone employed by the company doing the hiring. This is a person with a fat stack of resumes and a phone, whose goal is to whittle that stack down to a manageable level. Typically, the interview is brief. In some interviews, your general phone voice and manner are assessed. In others, the interviewer may be looking for the "right" answers to specific questions. In either case, this is not a time to discuss salary or other job specifics that are the province of someone higher in the chain of command.

The group interview

Phone interviews are often conducted by more than one interviewer at a time. Addressing yourself to a group of strangers can get confusing. Silly as it may seem, you can clarify things by paying attention when introductions are made and drawing a picture of the people at a virtual table, complete with smiley faces or stick figures if the mood strikes. Write down the people's names and put yourself at the table. You can then address individual interviewers as things proceed. Since this is invariably a speakerphone experience, one disadvantage of a group interview is the potential that you will have difficulty hearing your interviewers. Always ask for clarification if something is unclear.

The ambush interview

In an ambush situation, your interview is not scheduled for a specific time. Your phone will ring, and you will have no warning you are about to be interviewed. This puts you at a definite disadvantage, especially in light of all the things you can do to help yourself if you have some notice.

The best course of action is deferral. Politely explain that you are happy to get the call, impressed with the company, and interested in the job, but you cannot talk now. You're heading into a meeting, but you would be delighted to speak about the job later in the day or tomorrow.

The goal here is to secure a follow-up interview at a definite time. If there is any hesitation on the interviewer's part, volunteer some times that would work for you. Get the person's name and number. Offer to call or to be sitting by the phone at a designated time—just try to secure a commitment of a follow-up call in the near future.

Phone Interview Basics

At one time, it was a given that the person on the other end of the phone was not in a position to hire you. It was a preliminary contact. That person could cross you off the list of candidates, but there was no chance a job was in the offing during the phone interview. In the old days, nothing would happen without a personal appearance.

That is still true in many cases. Companies still do screening interviews in a variety of ways, but it is no longer a given that a phone interview is inconsequential. The job market, like so many markets, has gone global. Decisions can be made at long distance. The phone interview may turn out to be the final interview. It may be a preliminary interview that will be followed by yet another phone interview. There is simply no way to tell.

In other words, don't be lulled into thinking that the phone interview is a formality and you will inevitably be sitting in a room with your "real" interviewer. This may be as real as it gets.

Prepare just as you would for any interview. Expect the usual round of questions: "Tell me about yourself." "What are your strengths and weaknesses?" "Where do you see yourself in five years?" Rehearse your answers.

Emphasize your skills and accomplishments. Relate them to the company and its mission. Show the interviewer that you have done your homework. Be yourself. Be alert. Don't forget to breathe.

Be sure you have some questions ready for your interviewer. Make them open-ended. Use them to show your familiarity with the company and the industry, and to demonstrate sincere interest and enthusiasm.

So far, then, it's an interview like any other, but phone interviews have some special features that set them apart.

Projecting the Right Image

You know what to wear to an in-person interview, but what does that have to do with an interview in which no one can see you? The answer depends on your personal preference. Some people find that their mode of dress affects their state of mind, and they go all out. If a suit and tie helps you to get into a professional mind-set, don't hesitate to dress up. At the very least, consider wearing something presentable. Clothes can affect your self-image, and the right choice of outfit can help you project the right qualities. Do what works best for you.

Even though you can't be seen, smile. Strangely enough, smiling makes a detectable difference over the phone.

Another invisible factor that can make a difference in the impression you make is your position. You sound different slumping on the couch than you do sitting at a desk or standing while you talk. Standing can help you to make an especially active and engaged impression.

A Very Brief History of the Job

We can have jobs without interviews. There is no chicken and egg problem here, since the existence of a job is the absolute prerequisite, but historians and economists have had a lot to say about jobs through the ages and little to say about interviews. The origin of the job makes for a good—even unavoidable—starting point.

In the beginning, there was only one job: survival. Our roles were influenced by gender, with men doing most of the hunting and women most of the gathering. There were cultural exceptions, of course, but women's unique status as the bearers of children certainly affected the division of labor. Still, we can imagine some specialization. Perhaps someone cooked particularly delicious mammoth or had a knack for finding the homiest cave. As far as we know, though, no one was working for, or getting paid by, someone else.

We couldn't have jobs until we settled down, and we didn't settle down until we invented agriculture some 10,000 years ago with the Neolithic Revolution. At that point, we had to stay put. Crops need sowing, tending, and harvesting, and we began to cluster together in villages and towns.

Then we were able to specialize a bit, but it took one more revolution for us to take on the kinds of roles that an observer today would call jobs. About 6,000 years after agriculture began, we invented money. Currency replaced barter as the foundation of economic society. We no longer had to stay close to the sources of food, because we didn't have to worry about swapping with our neighbors. We could be paid for our work with a monetary symbol of stored value.

The job market, such as it was, was nothing like today's job market. Boys and girls followed in their fathers' and mothers' footsteps. On the farm, they were simply the younger generation that would inevitably take over the old homestead. Gender roles were distinct. If you were a boy and your father was a blacksmith, you succeeded him in due time. When there was no heir to take over, the blacksmith might take on an apprentice, and that was the route to working in a craft or trade.

Shortly after the turn of the 19th century, everything changed, at least in some parts of the world: the Industrial Revolution fired up its engines. The forces that had governed the settled agrarian societies of the planet for 10,000 years were about to be turned on their heads.

Before the Industrial Revolution, the greatest economic danger for a society was reproductive success. Resources were limited to begin with, and spreading scant resources over an increasing population was a recipe only for increased misery. Peace, health, and order were society's enemies in those days. We may not have understood or acknowledged it, but we counted on war, pestilence, and famine to keep the population under control, especially the population of those at lower economic levels.

The rich, meanwhile, could afford to reproduce at much greater rates. Their descendants, however, were still forced to share in the same limited pool of resources, and this led to a sort of downward mobility. The progeny of the upper classes, better educated than their inferiors, had to participate in the economy, albeit in less exalted roles than their parents' generation. There was simply not enough to go around otherwise. This was a labor force in the making.

The Industrial Revolution allowed us to increase our resources as never before. In general, people grew more prosperous, especially because the increased resources were accompanied by a decline in fertility. Now, increased resources did not have to be stretched so far.

On the job front, the Industrial Revolution created the employment market we know today, but it could not have done so without the changes wrought by the Neolithic Revolution. We needed settled communities and disciplined labor forces in order to build and operate factories, and those conditions developed in agrarian societies.

Without those settled agrarians, these changes might never have happened. As an example, consider Australia, where agrarian settlements were not established until the arrival of European settlers at the very end of the 18th century. The arrival of those representatives of a settled agrarian society enabled the creation of an advanced economy where none had existed before.

Tools of the Phone Interview Trade

In case the interview turns out to be more than a brief screening, have some water close at hand. A full phone interview can easily last for 30 minutes, and, unless things go astray, you will be doing a lot of talking.

Decide on the kind of phone you want to use. If you have the option, a landline has some advantages, despite its archaic origins. Landline connections are solid, and their voice quality is almost always superior to even the best cell phone reception.

If you do not have access to a landline, get your cell phone in shape for the interview beforehand. Be sure it's charged and silenced. The last thing you need in an interview is distraction, and cell phones are marvels at seeking your attention when you least want to be interrupted. If signal strength varies at the location where you expect to take the call, bear that in mind when selecting the ideal spot.

Silence is also the goal for all the other beeping and buzzing pieces of technology that surround most of us today. Turn it all off for the duration of the interview.

Distraction and noise can come from other sources, too. Children and pets are high on that list. Find a place where you can anticipate a modicum of privacy, and let people know that you are going into "do not disturb" mode when the call is expected.

Once all that is in place and you're ready to settle into your private, distraction-free space, the next question is whether or not to use a speakerphone. The advantage is obvious: you have your hands free for taking notes or referring to any materials, including online resources, that might be helpful. The disadvantage is equally clear: sound quality often suffers.

The best thing to do is to conduct a test before the call. If you can find a willing partner, try out different options and solicit some feedback. Do some practice runs standing and sitting, smiling and serious, with and without the speaker. Another excellent option is to use a headset. Again, make sure you are comfortable with your setup well in advance.

A good number of phone interviews are conducted by more than one person at the employer's end, so you're likely to be on their speaker no matter what.

Your comfort is crucial. If you are uncomfortable standing during the call, take a seat, even if you sound a little better when you stand. Phone interviews can produce enough anxiety all by themselves, without your making choices that are simply wrong for you personally.

Handy Materials

One of the great advantages of a phone interview is that it is an open-book test. You are allowed to have helpful materials close at hand.

Foremost among those materials is a copy of your resume. Interviewers will inevitably refer to it. If you submitted other materials with your application, have copies of those handy as well. If your resume refers to a particular document—whether a presentation, a study, or a portfolio—you may want to refer to it if the subject arises.

In second place, running very closely behind that copy of your resume, is a cheat sheet for the occasion. Some questions always get asked, and an outline of your answers can be very helpful. Don't make it so detailed that you end up reading it aloud, or so dense that it becomes a source of confusion. Keep it simple: bullet points and not paragraphs.

Three bullet points per answer should provide enough ammunition for the three utterly predictable interview questions: your strengths, your weaknesses, and, although it may come in one of several other guises, the chance to "tell us about yourself." In your outline, focus on specifics, describe particular situations, and try to connect your answers to the needs of the employer on the other end of the line.

A similar cheat sheet is enormously useful when your interviewer asks if you have questions. Drawing a blank here is simply not an option. It immediately sends a message: you are just not interested. Asking questions that relate to the wonderful things the company can do for you is almost as bad. Your questions need to focus on the things you can do for the company—not, for example, how soon you can head off on vacation.

Don't hesitate to rely on a computer, but don't let it become a distraction. Turn the speakers off and resist the temptation to click around the Web during the interview. You can, however, open your browser to the company site. If there is a page devoted to the company's mission statement, it can serve as a nice reminder of the appropriate context for your answers. If you can anchor your answers to aspects of that mission statement, you can make interviewers very happy.

Finally, set out a pad of paper and pen so that you can take notes.

During the Interview

That covers the preliminaries. You have a quiet, private spot. Your phone is charged. Your resume and notes are handy. There's a glass of water at your elbow and a mission statement staring you in the face.

Once the phone rings, is there anything else to remember?

Above all else, be conscious of the interview's tone. Some people are so used to phone conversations with their friends that they lapse into a sort of offhand informality whenever they're on the phone. The best interview is more conversation than interrogation, but it is still a relatively formal interaction. Courtesy matters throughout. Calling your interviewer by name when appropriate is an indication that you are engaged in the process. Your overall demeanor should be that of someone who is alert, thoughtful, and interested in the job, the company, and the industry. Reinforce that impression whenever possible.

Your invisibility during a phone interview allows you to refer to the materials you have gathered without anyone knowing, but your interviewer is invisible as well. Both parties are deprived of the useful social cues that are available in person in the form of body language. Those cues help ease interpersonal interactions when you are face-to-face. A shift in position or a change of expression can tell you when your interviewer is finished with a question. On the phone, there is significantly more guesswork involved.

You don't want to be interrupting your interviewer or answering partial questions before they are fully asked. To avoid this, pause before answering. Collect your thoughts for a second and be sure your interviewer is done before you leap in with an answer.

If a question takes you by surprise, or if it is complicated enough to require a bit of thought, ask for a moment. When you are in the same room, your interviewer knows you have heard the question and sees you giving it the consideration it undoubtedly deserves. On the phone, this pause translates into dead air. Avoid giving the impression that you have abandoned the call or fainted dead away. There is nothing wrong with needing a moment to deliberate. Even hiring managers sometimes need time to collect their thoughts.

Aside from the absence of body language, there are other ways communication can be compromised in a phone interview. Some interviewers fail to speak clearly. Some phones have their own problems with clarity, and those that do not can still be victimized by unreliable connections. If, for any reason, you cannot hear or understand what is being said, ask for clarification. You do not want to be forced to guess what you were just asked. Again, hiring managers know that phones are not perfect.

Occasionally, things get bad enough so that conversation becomes impossible. Your phone may be constantly cutting out so you hear parts of sentences, or one party cannot hear the other at all. Obviously, the situation has to be addressed.

Let your interviewer know about the problem and ask for an alternative. Perhaps you can get to another phone and continue from there. Perhaps the interview needs to be continued later. In that case, try to set a specific interview appointment instead of leaving things to a vague future that is all too easily ignored.

CHAPTER 5

The Only Question You Must Be Able to Answer

Not only strike while the iron is hot,
but make it hot by striking.
—Oliver Cromwell

The world is filled to the brim with job-hunting advice, and much of that advice purports to give the hapless job seeker a way to cope with interview questions.

The typical approach is to make a list. It's common knowledge that people like lists and always have, going all the way back to the Ten Commandments.

So in the interview advice section of any bookstore, we may see something like *The 10 Interview Questions You Must Know*—but this is only the beginning. He has 10 questions? Try my new book, *The Top 99 Questions*. Not enough? How about their latest, *More Than 199 Questions and Answers*?

But wait! Before you buy that, we have something better: *Millions of Questions and Billions of Answers.*

Mutually assured destruction is back, apparently, besetting the world of interview advice like the nuclear arms race beset the world for decades during the last century. Deterrence is not part of the picture here. The lists go on and there seems to be no end in sight.

Is any of this useful? Is your best bet a list of all the questions in all the interviews in all the conference rooms in all the countries in the world?

There are some slight exceptions, but I'll hold the disclaimers for a moment in order to give a very simple answer: no. You do not need to study 500 interview questions to ace an interview.

The reason you can avoid those hundreds of sample questions is that there is really only one question that matters. Everything flows from that one question. It will always be asked. It will make or break the interview. Answer that one question well, and your work at the interview is finished.

The precise wording of the question can change. It can be phrased in different ways, sometimes failing to arrive in the form of an actual question. Regardless of the choice of language or the tone of voice in which it is asked, it is the one offer you can't refuse. It is all you know and all you need to know. It's a simple phrase, but it can leave interviewees at a loss:

"Tell me about yourself."

Now, there is a place somewhere for those hundreds of other questions. No one should head into an interview completely unprepared for the usual suspects, but most of the predictable questions are so well known that they need no elaboration. It should not be a surprise that you might be asked about your strengths and weaknesses, even if you have never researched interview questions. The fact is that most of the questions, no matter how they sound, are variations on the "about me" theme.

When It's Not All About You

Do interviewers ever depart from the theme? Yes, but only to ask an entirely different form of question, one that is particularly popular among technology companies. There, the interviewer does not so much pose a question as lay out a problem. The job of the interviewee is to solve that problem, preferably while elucidating the thought process that leads to the answer.

To be blunt, preparing for those technical questions is impossible unless you know the questions in advance. It's safe to predict you will be asked something that relates to your field, and you will need to fall back on your accumulated knowledge to arrive at a solution. Your resume got you this far, though, and you have been working in this field successfully. You should know how to do certain relevant things. If you are asked a question about programming in Java and you don't speak that language, pre-interview preparation is no help. If you can learn a whole new language in a matter of days, and you know it will be on the agenda—even though, presumably, your resume makes no claim of relevant expertise—by all means prepare.

Otherwise, your education and your experience are your preparation.

Technology companies started another trend when they decided to ask "creative" questions. Those questions call on people to solve problems that are outside their career skill sets. "How would you test an elevator?" "How many windows are there in Manhattan?" "How many piano tuners are there in the world?"

All of these are no-right-answer questions, meant to demonstrate the applicant's thought process, though they sometimes seem more oriented toward proving the interviewer's cleverness than to offering much insight into the interviewee. Microsoft and Google use them, and, for better or worse, hiring managers in non-tech industries have adopted that style of question as their own. "If it's good enough for Google, why wouldn't it work for us?"

You can never know if your interviewer has added one of these questions to the list. If you do know, because you've heard that this company likes to ask out-of-the-box questions, you will still have no idea which question will be asked. Preparation is not going to help much, but there's no harm in consulting a list of similar questions to get a feel for the possibilities, and no harm in getting a feel for things by practicing a few answers.

With the exception of questions that ask you to perform a task and those that pose some quasi-philosophical conundrum, every question is asking that same thing: Tell me about yourself. It appears in other forms, of course, but nothing changes. What led you to apply for this job? What are your strengths and weaknesses? What are your qualifications? Why are you the right person for this job? Why are you here? Why should we hire you?

All of these questions ask you to sell yourself, but it's important to remember that there is a very specific context for that mission. That context is made up of the job you want, the company that is hiring, the industry in which the company operates, and, to some indefinable extent, the person doing the interviewing. That last variable will always be mysterious and out of your control. It matters, though, because people respond to each other unconsciously, and an interviewer and interviewee will react to each other for reasons neither party can articulate. That part is a crapshoot.

The other elements of the encounter, however, are well worth analyzing. Those elements dictate the best approach to the most basic interview dynamic: How do you ensure that your response to the quintessential interview question aligns with your interviewer's concerns?

To summarize, you have to respond to the ultimate request—"Tell me about yourself"—in a manner that makes a very convincing case in a very specific context.

That is a straightforward task, but the experts offer a multitude of approaches to completing it. Consider those strategies, by all means. The chronological approach, for example, in which you list the jobs you have held to date, is a popular option.

There is a better way. Its beauty is that it comes as a natural situational response to the entire context of the interview.

Talking to Your Resume

Think about what has happened to get you this far. Your education and experience, as you have outlined on paper, have made enough of an impression on this company to get you in the door. Your resume was the sales device that worked its magic, so let's make that the starting point.

What does your resume look like? Typically, it has a headline, a summary, and a list of core competencies. An outline of your professional experience follows, usually in reverse chronological order and including the positions you held and your key accomplishments in those positions.

Your resume has already told this company about you in a way that was clear and, judging by the fact that you are here for an interview, compelling. It follows naturally that you can capitalize on your resume's effectiveness by using it as a template for that ultimate "about me" interview question. In other words, you want to use something that has been proven to work.

I call this approach "talking to your resume."

How does it work? Your interviewer has seen your resume. In fact, there's probably a copy on the table. That document will be your guide.

When asked to talk about yourself, the interviewer is not expecting you to make a speech. You do not want the interview to become a one-sided conversation, with all the boredom and lapses of attention that implies. Be brief, so the interview resembles a real conversation, the kind of give-and-take that helps people to connect with each other. Your answer should conform to a structure, and a useful structure is the three-part form that is taught as part of expository writing classes at every level: introduction, body, and conclusion. You are telling your story.

This is obviously not the unexpurgated version of your tale. You will need to edit your story to meet very particular guidelines. Where do you find those guidelines?

The most direct version of the guidelines can be found in the job description. It tells you what the company expects from you in the job, and your answer should illuminate the ways in which you meet those expectations. It tells you what qualifications the company values, and your answer should make it clear that you have those qualifications in spades.

All of this should become apparent when you compare your resume with the job description. That exercise should tell you where you match the company's needs. Those areas should be your emphasis.

It's worth noting that you will get the best results from this approach when your resume is in the best possible shape. The closer it is to perfection, the more you can rely on it to conquer the interview.

What if you don't have a job description to work with?

This is where research pays off. From the very beginning of the application process, you should be on a fact-finding mission. You should be learning about the company, the industry, the job, and how those three things fit together. You should be tailoring everything you do to what you learn, beginning with your resume. That same research will tell you how to describe yourself in a way that fits the company's goals. You will essentially create your own job description.

Take time before the interview to compare your resume and the job description, self-created or otherwise, side by side. Emphasize the places where they intersect.

When the Interview is an Audience

Let's consider an example. There's an opening for a ceiling painter that sounds promising. Your resume has done its job and opened the door for an interview, but you know that ceilings are not your specialty. You will have to deal with that in the interview. You have painted a ceiling or two, though, so you may be able to make it work. You enter the interview room, which is quite the setting: lots of paintings, tapestries on the walls, and marble on the floor. Your interviewer introduces himself as Julius. You're already on a first-name basis. Everything is ready. The interview begins.

"Tell me about yourself, Mr. Buonarroti."

This is your cue for the introduction. You could start with something general and inoffensive. "I'm a good people person. I like to sculpt. I've done some architecture, and I also like to do some painting and work with color. I'd be happy if you called me by my first name, Julius. Most people call me Michelangelo."

That may be an answer, but it is not *the* answer. It fails to deliver the appropriate message. You want Julius to know that you are the right candidate and that you understand the company's needs and how you can meet them. Even if you haven't made ceilings a priority in the past, Julius wants to fill the position of ceiling painter.

Speak directly to that need in your introduction. "I'd be delighted to tell you about myself and my qualifications. The first thing I have to point out is that I am an accomplished, professional ceiling painter with a broad set of skills and achievements in that role. My skills are not limited to ceiling painting, but many of those skills have helped me paint ceilings well. These same skills have also helped me paint walls and canvases. I am accomplished in all these media, but many of my most prominent successes have been as a ceiling painter."

That introduction is brief and to the point. You know what Julius wants, and you have given him reason to think that you are the one who can deliver it. Everything you say should support the notion that you are the right person for the job. Everything in your introduction should be relevant to the job description.

Follow the introduction with the body of your answer. Here, as is so often the case, preparation goes a long way, especially as this is another time when you do not want to give a rambling speech that departs from the right-person-for-the-job script.

Before the interview, review your resume in order to find three of your core competencies—sometimes called skills or qualifications—that match the requirements of the job description.

See if you can take those three competencies and bolster them with an illustrative example or two.

"One of my skills is color selection. Color selection is enormously important in ceiling painting, as I know you are aware. I was in charge of color selection while painting the ceiling of a small church in a Tuscan village last year, and the IEEE selected that church for the Colorful Ceiling of the Year award. Another example of my color selection can be found in the frescoes that I did for Lorenzo de' Medici, one of which won Most Colorful Fresco of the Decade."

Once you have established one skill, move on to the next.

"Another skill of mine is team leadership. To paint an enormous ceiling like that of Saint Peter's, hypothetically speaking, is not a job that one person can do on his own. You need a collaborative team, and that requires leadership. I have led teams in each of my previous positions as a ceiling painter; and, thanks to my team leadership, I received promotions in each of my roles. I also developed processes and procedures for teams in my position as ceiling and fresco ombudsman for the Medici family. This document inspired great collaboration in dozens of murals in Florence and elsewhere, and it is still used today whenever a big job is undertaken."

You are consistently talking to your resume. Your interviewer may even be following along with resume in hand, noting these same points as you describe them. The emphasis is on citing a skill, but not citing it in isolation. Instead, each skill translates into a demonstrable benefit for the company. You want Julius to realize that your skills helped past employers, and you want him to conclude that those skills will benefit him.

Three is not a magic number. Give two or four core competencies if they suit the occasion. You can throw in an additional point or two if they are important and you have the time. Keep it simple, and adhere to the same principle of employer-related benefit: "Also, I studied for several years with Giotto. I learned 3-D drawing from the best, and I was awarded the Most Likely to 3-D prize." This kind of supplementary information can be particularly effective if your research has revealed, for example, that Julius is a particular fan of the three-dimensional approach that is all the rage in Rome these days. By talking to your resume, you can select the points most likely to resonate with your interviewer.

Now you can move on to your conclusion. In essence, it repeats the key point you made in your introduction. It tells the interviewer, in a sentence or two, that you are the right person for the job. That is always the message. "Those are a few examples of my skills and the ways I have used them to benefit my employers. To reiterate, though, the key point is that each of these skills highlights my accomplishments as a ceiling painter. I'd be happy to discuss other skills if you like."

By all means, accept an invitation to discuss other skills if one is forthcoming. Simply follow the strategy of talking to your resume and hitting the highlights that matter in this interview for this job.

You may have noticed by now that this strategy provides answers to all of those questions that are just different ways to invite you to talk about yourself. If asked to detail your strengths, talk to your resume just as you would when asked to explain what brought you to the interview.

It should be clear that this interview strategy does not contemplate a spontaneous performance. You should not make it up as you go along—quite the contrary, since the best way to approach an interview is with practice. Write out your answers and treat them as a script. Revise them as you practice, so they start to sound natural. As things progress, throw away the script and replace it with bullet points. Practice some more. Keep at it until you can throw away the list of bullet points. It can take a lot of practice to get from the verbatim recitation of written answers to the conversational tone that sounds like spontaneity. Invest the time, though, because that practice will pay off.

Good acting seems spontaneous. It looks unrehearsed. In fact, the opposite is true, and endless repetition precedes a compelling performance. When Jack Nicholson blurts out, "You can't handle the truth," it feels as though he just couldn't help himself, that this was an impulsive act. If anyone in the audience is thinking that Jack suddenly lost control and couldn't stop himself from getting angry, they are the ones who can't handle the truth. Paradoxically, rehearsal is what makes it possible to be immediate once the time comes to perform. David Mamet, whose work frequently has the sound of people making it up as they go along, summed up the phenomenon: "We prepare in order to improvise."

When you practice, especially when reading aloud, you will immediately know which parts of your answers sound stilted and unconvincing. Keep revising until you are comfortable with the words, and keep practicing until things flow. You may not be starring in a major motion picture and getting Nicholson-level money, but an interview is just as much a performance as any turn on stage or screen.

How to Go Wrong

If you practice your answer and remember to talk to your resume, you can avoid many of the mistakes that people make when asked to talk about themselves. Those mistakes often happen when an interviewee tries to improvise and misunderstands the interviewer's purpose.

The hard truth is that, despite having given you an open invitation to talk about yourself, the interviewer does not really care about you personally. This is not a chance to share your autobiography.

If you were born in a log cabin and studied by firelight when you weren't busy splitting rails, the only employer who cares is the one in the rail-splitting business, and those companies are few and far between today. The interviewer does not care to hear your life story. Jobs you held in the distant past, places you have lived, and personal details that are not directly relevant are all subjects that do not further your interests in the interview. All that matters is that you have the skills the company needs. Anything else is irrelevant.

Ruthless editing is the order of the day.

Remember, the interview is part theater and part sales presentation. Speak to whatever it is that the interviewer is buying. To borrow from the accumulated wisdom of sales professionals everywhere, every product or service can use a unique selling proposition, the celebrated USP that gets the buyer to buy what you are selling. It sets the product apart from the competition. By talking to your resume, you get to your own USP. After all, you will be focused on your resume's highlights and emphasizing the same strengths that attracted the company's interest in the first place. Why abandon your resume when it has worked so well?

An even worse approach is to answer the question with a question. The interviewee who asks, "What would you like to know?" is not going far. Such a question tells the interviewer that you haven't really given this process much thought and that, for whatever reason, you didn't see any need to get yourself prepared. The invitation, "Tell me about yourself," is not some interview secret designed to catch people off guard. It is an absolutely standard tactic. Interviewers like it because it is an open-ended question that gives you lots of room to shine or to crash and burn, and they can ask it before they have finished shuffling papers and getting comfortable in their chairs.

In the end, if you talk to your resume, mistakes are easy to avoid. Review your resume. Review the job description. Compare the two and look for points of intersection. Write out your answer. Practice saying it aloud. Revise it until it sounds natural, and keep practicing until you barely have to think about what you will say. Relax, because you are in great shape to answer the one and only question that you know you will be asked. You know this beyond any doubt, even an unreasonable one, and you know exactly what to say.

(Don't) Tell Me About Your Weaknesses

By swallowing evil words unsaid, no one has ever harmed his stomach.

—Winston Churchill

Every interview is different, but every interview is the same. There may be some unusual questions, even the occasional detour into the bizarre, but three questions are thoroughly predictable. In fact, they are so likely to be raised that, when the conversation turns to life's inevitabilities, they deserve equal billing with death and taxes.

Taking a page from basketball's Miami Heat, with its "big three" of LeBron James, Dwyane Wade, and Chris Bosh, here are the big three of the job interview:

- Tell me about yourself.

- Tell me about your strengths.

- Tell me about your weaknesses.

Every interviewee should see these coming. No one should be taken by surprise, and no one should ever consider, even for a fleeting moment, walking into an interview without well-prepared answers to the big three questions.

You might think interviewers bristle at answers that seem rehearsed. Interviewers are, by and large, no fools. They know full well that these questions are always asked. They know you know that as well. You know, or you should know, that your interviewer knows that you know.

It's a truth worth acknowledging. Your interviewer knows everyone asks these questions, and he knows that you will have anticipated them and, if you're serious, prepared your answers. If the questions take you by surprise, that alone speaks volumes about your attitude. You prove that you haven't taken the process very seriously, and that's not the attitude that tends to get an applicant to the next stage of the hiring process.

It should be clear, then, that you should prepare. This does not mean that you should drone on endlessly and deliver a monotonous recitation of a memorized script. It does mean you should think through your answers and practice your delivery.

Your Weaknesses

All three questions are important, but one of them is especially tricky: Tell me about your weaknesses.

This question is a trap.

To avoid falling into the trap, you must remember one thing about yourself, even though that one thing is patently false: for the purposes of the interview, you have no weaknesses.

Obviously, this is an outright lie. We all have weaknesses. Not one of us is perfect. Human beings are inherently flawed, some more than others, and we are just as flawed at work as we are in any other part of our lives.

This is not breaking news. It is not something that has somehow escaped the interviewer's notice over the years, and it is unlikely that the interviewer expects to spend his days evaluating a parade of superhuman candidates. You will not be asked to turn water into wine during the interview.

Is the right approach, then, to elaborate on your many foibles and idiosyncrasies? No, this approach misses the point.

The interviewer knows you are human. Therefore, he knows you have weaknesses. He also knows, however, that if you are a smart candidate, you will find a way to answer the question without disclosing those weaknesses—or, at least, those weaknesses that would be fatal to your prospects. You, being that smart candidate, will accommodate him. You will play the game by answering the question without actually answering the question.

You might be tempted to throw some real weaknesses out there because they seem trivial or innocuous. Resist. You run the risk of showcasing exactly those weaknesses that are worrying the employer. Unless you can read the interviewer's mind, you are perilously close to falling into the very trap that the question has set. You can, however, talk about actual weaknesses if you frame them properly, and the result may be an answer that sounds more honest and still does you some good.

The Usual Suspects

Unless your interviewer is new to the job, there are some answers she has heard at least a thousand times before. These are the kind of answers that probably occurred to people who were interested in joining the pyramid-building team being assembled by Tutankhamen, and people still use them all too often.

The classic example is "I'm a perfectionist," followed closely in popularity by "I work too hard."

There are two problems with this type of response. First, the answer is meaningless. It is obvious that the applicant is mouthing something that sounds like a weakness, at the same time expecting the interviewer to recognize that it's really a fabulously desirable strength. The answer is disingenuous at best, but that's not all that's wrong. The second problem is that it gives the interviewer clear and convincing evidence that the applicant has not given the process much thought. If you weren't willing or able to take the interview seriously, how likely is it that you will approach your job with a better attitude?

Once you have admitted to your horrible perfectionism, do not expect the interviewer to be stunned into silence by the blinding realization that this flaw of yours is exactly what the company needs. That will not happen.

Your interviewer, having reviewed your paperwork and spent a few minutes chatting, has probably noticed at least four of your unacknowledged flaws already. Amazingly enough, perfectionism is not among those flaws, but your interviewer is ready with more questions. She may ask for a concrete example of the terrible consequences of your alleged flaw. She may ask you to describe some more of your weaknesses. Whatever happens next, be prepared, because your first answer did not get you very far.

Another option, of course, is to take the plunge and simply say that you have no weaknesses. That choice may seem to make a certain sense in context, since it aligns so well with the apparent goal of convincing the interviewer that you are free of faults, but the goal is actually slightly different. The real goal is to present yourself as a human being complete with flaws, but one whose weaknesses need not trouble someone who makes hiring decisions.

What Do Interviewers Want?

Bear in mind that your interviewer has heard it all before. The phony, too-good-to-be-true answers have all been tried. They have failed, but not only because they are inherently unconvincing. On one level, they also show that a candidate has not given the interview much thought. An interviewer will be tempted to extrapolate from that thoughtlessness, wondering if the applicant has the capacity to think critically about his own performance.

One thing interviewers want, then, is a candidate with some level of self-awareness.

In addition, many interviewers see the question as a way to evaluate the applicant's ability to think creatively and to perform under pressure. Admittedly, this is something of a stretch, since everyone sees—or should see—the question coming.

There is also a school of thought that sees the question as a mistake, the equivalent of asking the candidate for reasons to choose someone else for the job. That school holds that there is a qualitative difference between asking for a simple statement of your weaknesses and asking for a description of work situations that have given you trouble in the past, along with a summary of how you dealt with them.

As a result, interviewers have learned to vary the phrasing of the question. Instead of asking you to talk about your biggest weakness, they try different approaches. "What would your last manager say about ways in which your work could improve?" "What areas of your performance are you working on?"

Sometimes, the approach is more specific. "Think of three situations that you found difficult and tell me what you did to overcome those difficulties." "Tell me about a project that did not go as expected, and describe what happened and how you responded."

All of these are simply variations on the weakness theme, and none of them requires a whole new approach. In fact, if you develop an effective strategy for even the simplest version of the question, you should be able to deal with variations without breaking a sweat.

Any strategy you use should recognize the question in its many forms and respond to it in a way that addresses the interviewer's concerns. As long as your answer does those two things, you have some latitude in choosing your specific approach.

From Out of the Past

Beginning with the proposition that you are not about to sabotage your own interview by discoursing on your real weaknesses, all that is left is to talk about your strengths.

You can tilt the conversation in the right direction by describing something that seemed like a weakness when you first confronted it. You were not sure that you were up to the task, but you learned something by overcoming your concerns.

"Describe something that has given you trouble at your job."

"Hmmm, great question. I really think I have the skills and experience for this job. Perhaps early in my career I was a bit too ambitious about taking on tasks. Back when I was with Company X, my manager came to me after a week and asked if I could handle part of a presentation in addition to my regular job, because someone had just left and the company was in a bind. Well, maybe I should have turned him down because it seemed like a daunting task, but I wanted to be helpful. And that taught me just how much I can accomplish when I set my mind to it. It may not have been the most perfect presentation, but it got the job done, and I ended up learning an area that had been unfamiliar to me."

The answer deals with a weakness that turns out to be illusory, while emphasizing a willingness to take on new things and go the extra mile.

The particular weakness is irrelevant. What matters is that you have dealt with the problem.

"Tell me about your weaknesses."

"When I first started out, I had trouble sorting out a good balance between life and work. I realized that my time management skills needed improvement and that my unbalanced approach wasn't best for my family, my employer, and me. I decided to get a better handle on things, and I devoted a lot of energy to developing better ways to manage my projects and my time. For the past two years, I have settled on a system that combines my calendar and all my project information. That system allows me to break things down into discrete chunks, make reliable forecasts of project timing, and allocate my resources realistically. At the same time, I joined a gym and started a healthy diet. Those changes have served me well, and I'm in much better shape, at work and at home, because I'm more in control of all the competing demands that everyone faces."

A Very Brief History of the Job Interview: The Baroque Era

Interviews must have always been a part of obtaining employment through anything other than accident of birth. No interview was needed if you were born into a family of serfs. Your fate was sealed. Born the son of a blacksmith, your career was chosen for you. Should the blacksmith be without male heirs, apprenticeship was the solution, and selection could hardly have been random. A prudent blacksmith would hardly take on an apprentice he hadn't even met.

When we look back in time, though, evidence of that kind of interview is conspicuously absent. Literacy was rare. No one was keeping records. There were no best practices. Human resource consultants were not roaming the medieval landscape, offering advice and hosting seminars.

In general, no one cared to keep records; if they cared, they lacked the necessary tools. Thus, the historical record is almost completely blank.

There were at least some small exceptions, though. Some positions were not everyday jobs. For one thing, they were desirable enough to engender competition. For another, they were considered important by those doing the hiring, and filling one of those important positions was serious business.

In the 1600s and 1700s, one of those important and competitive fields was music, at least partly because music was tied closely to religion. The music business then was hardly the business we know today. Musicians—or, more accurately, musician-composers—were employed by churches, noble courts, and towns, with frequent overlap among the three. Along with its use as entertainment, music had a place in the liturgy and in the celebration of local occasions. Civic authorities had formal processes for the selection of musicians, and, like governments everywhere and always, they kept written records of their activities. Their successors preserved those records. As a result, music is one of the few occupational categories in which evidence of employment practices has survived.

Getting a musical job was not simply a matter of hereditary appointment, despite the existence of musical lines such as the Bach family. In fact, we would still recognize some of the practices employed to find and hire a new court composer, including the way in which openings were publicized.

Employers of musicians were among the first to use newspaper advertising to attract applicants. In 1763, a newspaper in Kassel, Germany, ran the following ad: "The laudable Hessian Leib-Dragoner-Regiment requires an oboist who can play oboe, transverse flute, and clarinet and who possesses good references. The applicant should contact the above regiment at Kirchhayn."[1] A job description! References! Contact information! With the addition of an equal-employment-opportunity banner, the ad could run in today's *New York Times*.

The typical application process was also something today's applicant would recognize. If you wanted to apply, you would send along a cover letter and some letters of recommendation. You might enclose samples of your work, in the form of printed compositions, in the hope of impressing your prospective employer.

Inevitably, there were auditions, but there could be other hurdles.

One of the giants of the Baroque period, Georg Philipp Telemann, director of music for the city of Hamburg from 1721 until his death in 1767, added his own wrinkle to the process. Telemann supplemented the standard audition with a questionnaire. Its 12 questions covered music theory, the relationship between different musical styles, and the proper duties that attached to the position in question. With a bit of tweaking, that could work as a Google interview: a demonstration of some coding skill; some general questions about the company and the industry; and further questions about how the candidate sees himself doing the job.

Anyone skeptical of the questionnaire's value may have a point. There is a school of thought that claims Telemann had ulterior motives, especially with respect to one candidate, Conrad Friedrich Hurlebusch. Hurlebusch was an applicant for the job of organist and would serve under Telemann's supervision if hired. Though largely forgotten today, Hurlebusch was known during his lifetime as a fine musician and composer, if not a competent player of musical politics.

Hurlebusch was something of a prima donna, a man with a prickly demeanor and a history of turning down other positions. Telemann knew all this. Hurlebusch's reputation preceded him, and it did not endear him to the august director of music.

In an essay called "Naïve Questions and Laughable Answers: An Eighteenth-Century Job Interview," musicologist Steven Zohn has this to say about Telemann and his interview with the difficult diva: "One therefore wonders whether this line of questioning was intended to provoke Hurlebusch into giving inappropriate responses that would eliminate him from consideration. In other words, Telemann, being faced with the prospect of having to hire a musician who was both the most qualified and the least congenial, may have purposely designed the interview to extricate himself from a delicate political situation."[2]

In the end, Hurlebusch treated the "degrading" interview with contempt, and, as he put it in his 1740 autobiography, "they were left to offer their organ to someone else."[3]

Job seekers today can be forgiven for thinking that Telemann's interview served as the model for all interviews that followed. It speaks of a job market doing its best to convince you that you'll never be right for the job.

That suspicion is not unheard of in nonmusical realms. Michelangelo may not have had an interview, per se, for that Sistine Chapel job—he was, by that time, a known quantity. But, by his own account, he was offered the work at the suggestion of artistic rivals. As he saw it, those rivals recommended him in the hope that, since the job entailed working in a medium unfamiliar to him, Michelangelo would fail. One of those rivals, Raphael, would look better by comparison.

Modern historians discount the truth of the story, seeing it only as a reflection of Michelangelo's own attitude. His skepticism does seem unhappily consistent with the negative feelings of many job seekers in many markets through the years. Your interviewer may not be out to get you, but a bad experience or two can make you wonder. Both Hurlebusch and Michelangelo would understand.

A Work in Progress

Not every weakness you mention in an interview has to be a thing of the past, as long as you don't present it as something that is currently out of control despite your best efforts. The two keys are that you demonstrate your awareness of a particular weakness and describe the steps you are taking, and have taken, to get it under control. It is perfectly acceptable to still need to take those steps. It is not acceptable to let a weakness grow unchecked.

This is another time when the subject matter of your answer is of little consequence unless the weakness has special relevance to the job requirements. In other words, if the job requires someone with a commitment to obsessive accuracy, and you have a problem with getting details right, it may be time to look for other opportunities. It is certainly not the time to confess your tendency to approach your work too casually.

Here, the best answers come in two parts. They require some actual awareness of your flaws and some attempt to remedy them. Part one is devoted to a description of the weakness. Part two is a description of your response.

In other words, you're talking about a real weakness that you have worked on and that may still be something you need to watch. A weakness then becomes a skill, even if there is still room for improvement.

Some examples:

"When I moved from General Stuff to Amalgamated Widgets a few years ago, there was one part of my job that was new to me, and it was the one part I didn't enjoy. I tended to put that task off until the end of the day. That meant there were days when I hadn't allowed myself enough time to finish the job; and, because of that, I didn't always produce my best work in that one area. It also meant that the rest of my day was impacted by the knowledge that I would need to tackle that task. The best approach for me, I learned, was to do that kind of task first. This meant I had enough time to do it well and that my approach to the rest of the day was much more positive. Even now, I occasionally have to remind myself to tackle those tough jobs first, so I still order my priorities with that in mind."

"Around three years ago, when I was at International Mulch, I realized that email could be a problem for me because of its potential to distract. I would be focused on a project and really in the zone in terms of productivity, but I couldn't help but be distracted any time my computer notified me that new mail had arrived. I'd check, and then I would have to refocus on the work I'd been doing. Some messages are important and some are even urgent, but not all of them needed my immediate attention. I've set up my system using rules that help filter the important mail from the rest, and I stopped allowing my computer to notify me of each and every message. The important stuff still gets my attention, but I don't need to obsessively check. I've found that it's worth applying the tools that suit an individual's working style. In my case, dealing with ongoing distractions is important for my productivity."

"I have a tendency to be impatient, so I never really liked training new staff. The more I've done it, though, the more I've found it can make you look at things with fresh eyes and that you understand things better when you try to teach others. At this point, I value the opportunity to train new staff, and, even though I can still be a little impatient, it has been a learning experience for me, too. Just last month, I was asked a question about the way we manufactured our jet-propelled skateboards, and it gave me an idea of how to streamline the process."

The advantage of this approach is that you are telling the truth. You do have weaknesses, but you are aware of them and have taken steps to turn them into strengths. For many interviewers, the most important factors are your awareness of your situation, your willingness to improve, and the fact that you have taken concrete steps to raise your game.

Few interviewers will be taken aback by the idea that you have not been able to make some flaw vanish entirely. Instead, this kind of answer comes across as thoughtful, genuine, and, best of all, credible.

Credibility

One of your obvious goals is to give answers that the interviewer finds truthful. You are not answering under oath, and you are not about to reveal the kind of real weaknesses that are likely to derail your candidacy, but vague answers conjured out of the ether will not be convincing. If nothing else, they invite your interviewer to ask for an example of how a particular weakness played out in real life.

Anything you say will be more convincing if it is part of a story. A story has a beginning, middle, and end, and it is brought to life by its details. A story grounded in real events will always trump an answer that amounts to a recitation of platitudes.

This is where preparation pays off. Think of a weakness and think back to a time when you took action to correct it. Put it in context:

"When I was assistant manager at Amalgamated Widget three years ago, I realized I was having trouble getting things to ship on time. Everything was happening at the last possible minute, when panic would set in because of the looming deadline. No one had taken the time to break projects down into their component parts and assign realistic time frames to each part. Instead, we would get an assignment and a deadline. I found that I needed a system that would assign time frames to separate parts of the process. Since there wasn't something already in place, I set to work developing that system. It didn't fix things immediately, and I found that it had to be revised and amended as time went on, but it ultimately allowed us to deliver work on time, with less panic and fewer mistakes. That system helped our team earn company awards for reliability in 2010 and 2011."

The Obvious Weakness

There are some situations in which your choice of subject matter is made for you. Before you even get to the interview, you know that there is some aspect of your career that is likely to be on your interviewer's agenda, and this is your one chance to be a successful mind reader.

If you can point to an aspect of your resume that you just know is going to come up, the best approach is to meet it head-on. Don't wait for your interviewer to broach the subject. That only makes it look as if you are avoiding the issue or, in some cases, that you are disturbingly unaware of it.

This situation often arises when the candidate is making a big change. A change in career field needs to be acknowledged. A change in responsibility, such as when you are applying for a position with significantly more or less responsibility than your previous jobs, should also be addressed. You may be overqualified or underqualified, but your resume has gotten you in the door.

When talking about this kind of weakness, don't put the onus on the interviewer with a statement that makes her the source of concerns. Don't cast her as the opposition by saying, "I would imagine that you are concerned about my lack of experience in this specific field."

Instead, treat her as an ally and put the source of concern outside this conversation. "Someone might think that I haven't had enough exposure to this part of the job, and that's understandable, but they may not be giving enough thought to the parts of my career that are really relevant to this issue." Proceed to make your case, in detail, to that skeptical "someone."

If this kind of weakness applies to you, you are probably all too aware of it already. Your self-appraisal is likely to be accurate, even though many of us do tend to be our own worst critics. This answer, above all the rest, takes practice, but it's not terribly different from describing a weakness and then explaining why it's not an issue.

None of this means, however, that you should volunteer a weakness that is obvious to you but fatal to your chances. If the position involves making endless rounds of cold calls, your pathological shyness should not be the focus of conversation even if the problem is obvious to you. Of course, you should be asking yourself if this job is right for you at all, but that is an entirely different question, one better asked before you have gotten this far.

Back to Backboards

We began this chapter with the "big three" in interview questions and basketball players, and another look at basketball explains the right way to answer "Tell me about your weaknesses."

Suppose you are interviewing a remarkably talented player, someone with some great skills but a weakness in his game. In this case, he's a guard. He's quick, plays good defense, and handles the ball with superhuman grace. He's a scorer, too, but most of his points come from driving to the basket. His reputation is that his jump shot has been a weakness, and observers agree that he won't be one of the greats without improving that part of his game.

"Tell me about your weaknesses," you say.

His first answer: "I'm a perfectionist."

This is hardly the answer you were hoping to hear. If it means that he tries hard to do things at the highest level, it is not much of a weakness. It is the equivalent of telling you that he has no weaknesses. If it is the best answer he has for you, it shows that he does not have much awareness of his performance in the workplace.

As the interviewer, you may find yourself tempted to roll your eyes.

Instead of giving up, you decide to follow up with something else. "That sounds a lot like a strength. Can you tell me about another weakness?"

This time, the player, having remembered reading the advice in this chapter, recalls the first strategy.

"When I first got into the league, I didn't have much of a jump shot. My coach, though, had designed a play that left me with the ball about fifteen feet from the basket. If the play went the way it was supposed to, I would be left unguarded. I was supposed to shoot. Coach was in love with the play and ran it over and over again. Even though jump shots were not the best part of my game, I accepted the responsibility. In the end, I found I could fake the shot and drive to the basket. I scored a lot of points that way, and that's one reason I became one of the best penetrating guards in the league. I realized I could make something good out of any play, even if the play was not something I was used to."

That answer is an improvement. At least it responds to the question, even if it changes the subject to one of the player's strengths. As an interviewer, you get some sense that the player has given a bit of thought to his game. There is hope.

The player could have taken the second approach and talked about a weakness that was real, that he understood, and that he has addressed. That does not necessarily mean that he has solved the problem, only that he is moving in the right direction.

"I've never had the best jump shot, but I was able to compensate for it with my quickness and ability to get to the hoop. We would run plays designed to get me open from fifteen feet, and I would fake the shot and drive to the basket. This usually worked, but I started to realize that a good jump shot would make me a more complete player. I started noticing that defenders were not going for the fake as much as they had, so it became harder to use my natural skills. I was too predictable. I started spending more time at the gym practicing my shot. I also spent a lot of time analyzing film so that I could spot the flaws in my shooting motion, and I got additional coaching. My shooting has improved, and I'm now hitting almost half my shots. I know that I can do even better, but I have to keep on top of things to make sure that I don't let my old habits take over. That's why I'm still at the gym for an hour after everyone else has gone home."

That is the kind of answer that warms an interviewer's heart. It's clear, it tells a story, and it shows awareness and initiative. It's not complicated, and it does more than list a series of amorphous qualities that could apply to everyone and no one.

Chapter 7

How to Succeed in a Panel Interview

*To think like a wise man, but to express
oneself like the common people.*

—Motto of playwright Lady Gregory,
based on Aristotle

It's one thing to walk into an interview and find one stranger sitting across the table. It can be quite another to be faced with a group of strangers who are all there to sit in judgment of your potential to be an asset to their business.

If the trial-by-panel approach doesn't make you nervous, congratulations are in order, but most of us are at least mildly intimidated by the prospect. The one-on-one rapport that can develop in the individual setting is harder to establish in front of a group—but the group interview has many things in common with the individual variety, and you can apply many of the same strategies to both settings.

Why a Panel?

Group interviews have a long history in academia, perhaps because academic institutions are made up of departments that are somewhat autonomous and seem to relish any opportunity to establish a committee. Thus, the hiring process is often managed by a search committee staffed by members of the department, sometimes accompanied by a representative from the general administration. Intra-faculty competition can make people anxious to participate in decisions that will affect the future of the department and, therefore, their individual careers.

Perhaps another reason the group interview is embraced in academia is because it's a familiar setting at the university. A doctoral candidate is often required to offer a defense before submitting her dissertation to the institution. In many universities, the defense consists of an oral presentation before a committee of experts, generally drawn from the departmental faculty, followed by a session of questions and answers.

Business has taken to that model, but there are some differences. Presentations are rarely required, except occasionally in interviews for scientific, technical, and sales positions. And unlike a doctoral candidate, who already knows most, if not all, members of the panel, a job interviewee faces a group of complete strangers.

A group interview has some clear advantages. It takes less time than an equivalent number of serial individual interviews. It puts all the interviewers on the same page, with each getting to evaluate the same answers to the same questions at the same time. It allows each interviewer to focus on his or her specialty, with less time devoted to pleasantries and small talk. It also exposes the candidate to what some see as a more pressured situation.

Panels had typically been reserved for the candidate's second or third interview, since it takes some work to assemble a group and reconcile conflicting schedules. More and more, though, companies are opting to convene a committee at the start. Your resume and other documents will be scrutinized, and there may be phone interviews to weed out the applicants who are less compelling, but a group interview as your first face-to-face encounter should not come as a shock.

Research

Research is essential for any interview, and a group interview is no exception. If anything, your research should be even more thorough.

You should know enough to put yourself in the shoes of the interviewers, and that is a good place to be, because their perspective can serve as your guide to the interview. Why do they want to meet you? What was it about your resume that made this company think you would be a good fit? If you can identify the strengths that captured their attention, you have a basis on which to focus when preparing answers to the questions you think they will ask.

Research the basics

Be sure you know where you are going and how you will get there. Leave yourself plenty of time. A panel is even less receptive to lateness than an individual interviewer, and you don't want to arrive at a room filled with fuming inter-viewers. If you can get some information on style of dress from within the company, by all means use it. Otherwise, a professional look is mandatory for any interview.

Research the people

Some companies will volunteer information about the interviewers, and there is nothing to prevent you from asking, with great politeness, who will be at the meeting. If you get that information, find out what you can about the people you are about to meet. You can find information on the company's website. LinkedIn may add more, and Google is always worth consulting.

Research the company

You would do this for any interview, and it should have been part of your application process from the beginning, when you tailored your presentation to company specifics. There is no such thing as too much preparation in anticipa-tion of a group interview, and you will certainly be relying on your company research when considering the content of the interview itself.

Preparation

Since the best preparation requires you to see yourself as others see you, your job is to take an objective look at your application. There is good news, to be sure: You have already impressed this prospective employer with your qualifications, and you are not burdened with weaknesses so glaring that your application went directly to the shredder.

Not all the news is good, however, and it is equally important that you think about your imperfections. If you were on the other side of the table, what would you look for in the perfect candidate for the job? Remember that there will probably be at least one member of the interviewing group who knows your field at least as well as you do. What might be on that person's wish list if he were building the perfect candidate? Where do you fall short of that superhuman ideal?

These do not have to be major flaws. Perhaps the company is looking for someone with several years of experience in three different programming languages, and you've only been working in Ajax for a year. Clearly, this was not enough to disqualify you, but it's likely to come up in the interview. You should be prepared for that.

You may also be asked about something you do not see as a flaw at all. For example, your employment history shows that you were at one job for a relatively short time. It is obvious to you that you left that position for the best, most understandable reasons. Those reasons may not be quite so obvious to one of your interviewers. Again, don't be taken by surprise. Prepare by reviewing your application with a skeptical eye.

Even in a group interview, you should expect to field the same questions that individual interviewers are notoriously fond of asking, such as:

- Tell us about yourself.

- What are your strengths and weaknesses?

- Where do you see yourself in five years?

- What did you like most about your last job?

- What did you like least?

- Why are you leaving your current job?

- Why do you want to work here?

Although those questions are the very heart and soul of the traditional interview, you should also be prepared for a completely different style of question, one that often comes into play when a group is doing the asking.

Situational and Behavioral Questions

The fact that interviews have not been shown to have much predictive power in relation to subsequent job performance has not made the interview less important or less popular among employers. It has, however, made employers more receptive to conducting structured interviews.

In theory, at least, a structured interview avoids some of the subjectivity inherent in the traditional panel interview format, where different interviewers ask different questions and grade the interviewee's performance on different scales.

In structured interviews, candidates are asked questions that are either behavioral or situational, and all interviewees are asked the same questions. When the technique is used in group situations, all interviewers are hearing the answers at the same time. Presumably, interviewees do not have to worry that they caught an individual interviewer on a bad day and that they are paying a price for that bit of unfortunate timing.

Behavioral questions ask about specific situations that candidates have encountered in the past. They focus on actual behavior in the workplace. Some examples:

- Describe a situation that you found highly stressful and what you did to manage it.

- Tell us about a time when you had to make a difficult decision.

- Describe a time when you set a goal and achieved it.

- Describe a time when you were unable to meet a goal you had set.

- Give us an example of how you have dealt with a specific conflict at work.

A good answer to one of these questions will include a specific description of an event, a description of the action or actions you took in response, and a statement of the result you achieved, what you learned from the experience, or how the situation was resolved.

Because behavioral questions ask candidates to recount actual events, every interviewee will tell a different story. As a result, it can still be difficult for interviewers to draw accurate comparisons between candidates.

Situational questions ask each interviewee to respond to the same story. In essence, they are hypotheticals. Instead of asking about the past, they ask you to describe what you would do if you were confronted with a specific set of facts. Examples include:

- In a department meeting, your manager brings up a project that has not gone well. She attributes the problems to decisions for which she holds you responsible. You feel this is not justified and reflects a lack of information on your manager's part. Her criticism seems unfair. What do you do?

- What would you do if a problem arose at work and you disagreed with the way your supervisor told you to handle it?

- You are responsible for a project with an imminent deadline. Just when the project is due, you realize that the work you have to deliver is flawed. How do you handle it?

To be effective, your answer to such a question should follow the format that applies to behavioral questions. Describe the specific steps you would take and the results you would expect. Think about alternatives and different approaches, and the benefits of each, revealing some of the thought processes that contributed to your answer.

Answers to situational questions do not have to be divorced from reality. In fact, some of the best use actual events. Start by addressing the hypothetical situation, but shift gears if you can think of a true story that parallels the fictional one. For example, if you are asked how you would handle a difficult colleague, do not hesitate to tell a true story of an actual difficult colleague and the steps you took to manage the situation effectively. Stories from real life make better examples than what-ifs. In this context, of course, the only stories you should tell are those with happy endings.

Both behavioral and situational questions invite follow-up. Be prepared to handle questions about why you took the steps you chose and about the relative virtues of alternate approaches. In addition, be prepared to respond to further hypotheticals that can be derived from your answer: "What steps would you have taken if your first approach had not worked?" "What made you choose the action you selected?" "Why didn't you try some other specific option?"

You cannot predict the exact questions you will be asked, especially once you get past the usual run of standard openers, such as the invitation to discuss your strengths and weaknesses, your plans, and your vision of the job. You should certainly practice your answers to those questions, but you should also formulate some of your own behavioral and situational questions. Think of the kind of questions that would apply to the qualities the company values in someone doing the job you are applying for.

If the job entails a great deal of customer interaction, for example, think of questions about managing that kind of relationship. If working as part of a team is important, focus your attention on questions that relate to colleagues, managers, and staff you would be supervising.

When you have devised a list of questions that relate to the position you're applying for, practice your answers aloud. Work toward answers that follow the situation-action-result structure, and try to ground your responses in specifics. You may not know what you will actually be asked, but it is well worth getting comfortable with the form that your answers should take.

For best results, practice with someone. First explain the concept of behavioral and situational questions. Let the person make up some samples, and practice with questions you haven't heard before. It doesn't matter if the questions are a little off the mark. What matters is that you have the chance to improvise, just as you will have to in the interview.

Your Questions for the Panel

The research you have done about the company does more than prepare you to answer questions. It helps you ask questions of your own.

Almost every interview concludes with a chance for the applicant to ask questions of the interviewers. This is a golden opportunity, something that can be just as important as what has gone before.

Use your research to think of smart questions that show your interest in the company and your knowledge of its business. This is not the time to ask what the company can do for you. Good questions are not about when you'll be entitled to vacation time or whether you'll get a parking space close to the entrance.

You might ask about the company's plans in the face of some recent industry change or about the way it handles some particular facet of the work you hope to do. In no event should you arrive at the interview without a few good questions for the panel.

At the Interview

When the day arrives, be prompt, professional, and polite to everyone. That includes anyone you speak with, not just the members of your panel. Think of every person you meet as someone who can affect the hiring decision, because you can never tell who has that kind of influence.

Once the interview gets started, there are many things you can do to help it go well:

- Get names and titles. You will undoubtedly be introduced to the members of the panel. Try to remember that information, as it will help you to personalize your answers. It will also come in handy when writing thank-you notes after the interview.

- Take notes. Ask first if anyone minds, but most interviewers will respect your businesslike approach. You can jot down names and titles, adding a word or two to remind you of an individual's interests, which you can mention when you send a thank-you note. You might even make a quick diagram of who is sitting where, to jog your memory during and after the interview.

- Do not, however, bury your head in those notes. Your focus should be on the people in front of you.

- Talk to everyone. When answering a question, direct yourself primarily to the person asking it, but try to make eye contact with everyone on the panel.

- Ignore no one. Unless you have a genius for deciphering group dynamics, you will not be able to identify the person whose opinion carries the most weight. It may be the person who talks the most or the person who talks the least, so each member of the panel should get some of your attention.

- Call people by name if you can. Your notes can help here.

- Reinforce your positives. Questions often relate to one another, whether they are touching on similar subjects or following up on earlier questions. You can use this to your advantage by reminding the panel about the strengths you described in one answer and expanding on those strengths with a slightly different focus.

- Don't be afraid to ask mid-interview questions. A group interview tends to be more formal than an individual interview—but, ideally, it is still more conversation than interrogation. If you have a question that naturally follows from your answer, go ahead and ask it. Doing so can make for a more collegial interaction.

- Be prepared for different styles. Sometimes everyone on the panel asks questions, often according to their areas of responsibility. Other panels will assign all or most of the questioning to one member. Regardless of the style, talk to everyone—even, or especially, that one sphinxlike figure seated at a corner of the table.

- Ask for clarification if you must. It would be a mistake to think that interviewers are any more perfect than interviewees. There is such a thing as a bad question, and not only in the sense that some questions cannot legally be asked. A question can be a confusing mess. If you have listened thoughtfully and you truly do not understand, say so. It is better to ask than to launch into an answer and hope for the best. If it's a confusing question, chances are that your puzzlement is shared by one or more of your other interviewers.

As the interview comes to a close, take advantage of the opportunity to ask your own questions. If one of your questions speaks to the specialty of one member of the panel, direct your question to that person, calling him by name if you can.

Ask if there is anything else the panel would like to know, and thank everyone for taking the time and giving you this opportunity. Shake hands with everyone. If possible, get business cards, which will help you with writing thank-you notes.

After the Interview

If you aced the interview, think twice before cartwheeling your way down the hall. If you are crushed by how badly it went, hold your tears until you are safely away. In either case, take things with a very large grain of salt. Remember that your evaluation of your performance may bear no resemblance to the panel's assessment.

When the dust has settled, send a short note of thanks to each member of the panel. If you have gotten their names and titles, write personal notes. For an even better impression, refer to the interviewer's role, especially if you can mention something covered in the interview. For example, if one panel member talked about the company's method for managing long-term projects, thank that person for explaining that facet of the business. You do not have to elaborate, nor should you. A simple mention in passing is enough to distinguish you from the competition, even those members of the competition who remember to write thank-you notes in the first place.

You should also assess your performance. If you thought some of your answers were weak, that is the place to focus your energies in preparing for future interviews. Practice your answers to the questions that gave you the most trouble.

A group interview can be an intimidating experience. You're heavily outnumbered, and you don't know who is really running the show. You don't have many of those social cues that ease the conversation when it's one-on-one. Rapport is more difficult to build with a group.

With preparation, however, a group interview is a manageable experience, and the fact that you have taken the time to do the research and put in the practice gives you a real advantage over the competition.

CHAPTER 8

Where Does the Law Draw the Line?

As citizens of this democracy, you are the rulers and the ruled, the law-givers and the law-abiding, the beginning and the end.

—Adlai E. Stevenson

At first glance, it may seem that there should be a clear way to identify illegal interview questions, but the real world is never so accommodating. For one thing, employment law comes from more than one source. There are federal laws, state laws, and, in case that's not enough complexity, local laws, generally the province of cities big enough to promulgate their own regulations.

A question may be legal under federal law but forbidden by the state, yet the reverse is almost never true. If a question is banned by federal law, a state cannot make it legal.

The complication of the statutory scheme is only the beginning. Some questions can be legally asked but cannot be used to make a hiring decision, a situation that can leave interviewees scratching their heads.

You are unlikely to be considered paranoid if you're skeptical about the ability of a hiring manager to ask that kind of question and ignore the answer when decision time arrives. Hiring managers are human—all too human, some would say—and that's why these laws were passed in the first place. Despite that, they must somehow learn to make the distinction between a question that can be asked and used to evaluate the applicant, and a question that can be asked as long as the answer is immediately forgotten.

That is not the last of the complications. There is one more distinction to address: Some questions can be asked if the interviewer's motives are pure. They cannot be asked if the interviewer is asking for the wrong reasons.

How does this work? To take one example, an interviewer can indirectly ask about a disability to determine if the applicant can perform essential functions of the job, with or without accommodation. If the interviewer has any other reason for asking, the question is illegal.

Discriminatory Subjects

Since the legalities of interview questions get complicated quickly, the easiest way to approach them is to consider the areas that constitute illegal discrimination in a broad range of employment circumstances, not just in the job interview. Those areas make for a long list of topics that are off-limits:

- Race

- Religion

- Age

- Place of birth

- National origin

- Sexual orientation

- Family status

- Marital status

- Disability

- Criminal history

Although that list covers a lot of ground, it is not exhaustive. There are questions that do not pry into those areas directly yet fall afoul of the law by venturing into forbidden territory by an indirect route. At the same time, questions can touch on those troublesome areas without being illegal, and that is when the interviewer's purpose and motive become relevant.

The legality of a given question often depends on its subject.

Race
Questions and comments about race are always illegal, a prohibition that extends to veiled questions that could have racially relevant answers. For example, a question about an applicant's membership to an organization would be

illegal if the answer might disclose an applicant's race. On the other hand, an interviewer can legitimately ask about membership in professional organizations that are relevant to the job.

Religion
Religion is equally off off-limits. Interviewers cannot ask about an applicant's faith or membership in a religious denomination. It is legitimate, however, for an interviewer to ask about an applicant's ability to work according to a particular schedule that is relevant to the employer's business, provided that all applicants are asked.

Age
The only time an interviewer can legally ask about age is when the job requires the applicant to have reached a certain age before being hired. Interviewers cannot get around the prohibition by asking about the applicant's history, or inquiring into dates of schooling or service in the military.

Place of birth and national origin
Employers have the right to confirm that an employee can legally live and work in the United States, but they have no right to inquire into an applicant's birthplace or family circumstances. If it is relevant to the job, interviewers can ask about a candidate's fluency in different languages.

Sexual orientation
An applicant's sexual orientation is not a legitimate subject. Nor is it legitimate to ask a question that alludes to sexual

orientation without directly addressing it—for example, by remarking on styles of dress.

Family and marital status

Interviewers cannot ask about an applicant's marital status or family situation. Questions about child care and pregnancy are illegal, as are questions about the composition of an applicant's home. An interviewer can ask questions about the applicant's ability to meet job requirements, including legitimate scheduling demands, if those questions are asked of everyone.

Disability

Disability is a minefield for interviewers. The law prohibits discrimination on the basis of disability, but it acknowledges that certain disabilities may legitimately interfere with performance. It then requires that employers accommodate disabilities, if such accommodation is needed, by making appropriate arrangements that allow the disabled candidate to do the job. Thus, an employer cannot simply ask if a candidate is disabled or inquire into the extent of a disability. The employer can, however, ask if an applicant is able to perform the essential tasks of the job, with or without accommodation.

Criminal history

Background checks are a common part of the contemporary workplace, but that does not mean interviewers have license to ask about applicants' criminal history. They can ask if an applicant has ever been convicted of a crime, especially if a conviction bears some relation to the job. They generally cannot ask about arrests or time spent behind bars. It is not always easy to determine which questions are appropriate, since some may have a direct connection to the type of job in question. An employer who hires someone with a history of burglary as an in-home cable installer can face legal difficulties unrelated to employment discrimination if something goes criminally wrong on the job.

How to Respond

As you might expect, not all interviewers have taken the time to parse the regulations that govern their behavior. Most of them have the obvious missteps under control, so you are unlikely to find interviewers asking direct questions about your racial identity or religious affiliation.

That leaves plenty of room for questions that are slightly more subtle but equally problematic. An interviewer may mean well, of course, and hold the sincere belief, for example, that single mothers make bad employees. That belief may even have stemmed from the company's experience with someone who turned out to be a single mother and who was the worst employee in the company's history. None of that makes it any more appropriate for the interviewer to ask a female applicant if she is a single mother.

It may also be the case that an interviewer asks an illegal question when she really intends to ask something else. Perhaps the company works double shifts on Saturdays, and the interviewer wants to be sure that nothing will interfere with your ability to adhere to that schedule, "such as religious obligations." The company is genuinely uninterested in your religion per se. In that case, an illegal question about your religious beliefs could have been more artfully phrased as one about your availability to work on Saturdays, and the interviewer would have obtained the information she wanted without breaking the law.

To some extent, then, your choice of response may be governed by whether you think your interviewer really expects you to answer an illegal question. In some cases, your interviewer might be asking a legitimate question but phrasing it in a way that crosses the line. That can happen when your interviewer is inexperienced or simply inarticulate. The difference may affect how you answer.

There are, sadly, other factors that can influence your answer. A question may tell you that the interviewer is beset by the kind of prejudice you simply cannot abide, and your only option is to terminate the interview. On the other hand, you may be desperate: You need the job, you don't see many other options out there in today's market, and you feel forced to tolerate what would otherwise be intolerable. Can you afford to fight this battle?

Your answers will depend on your personal situation and your assessment of the interviewer, but you have several choices when deciding how to respond.

Answer the question

You can, of course, answer the question directly. This course of action does the least to disrupt the interview. If you have developed any rapport with the interviewer, you won't harm it with a simple answer, and it is highly unlikely that your interviewer posed the question to test your knowledge of employment law. He doesn't expect you to challenge the question's legality. If it helps, you can make the assumption that your interviewer didn't know any better and that the question was an innocent mistake.

Answer the real question

If you think there is a hidden question behind the interviewer's words, you can choose to answer that hidden question instead of the ostensible one. If your interviewer asks about your religion, for example, your knowledge of the company may allow you to infer the real concern: that you may not be available when the company needs you. Instead of answering directly, you might respond, "I know the company operates every day of the week, and there is nothing that would make it difficult for me to be available whenever I'm needed."

This approach does require you to look behind the curtain and find the appropriate concern that was couched in inappropriate language, another example of the value of knowing as much about the company as you can. Without that knowledge, it can be much harder to draw inferences from simple questions.

Answer with your own question

If you cannot imagine a legitimate reason for the interviewer asking an inappropriate question, and you would rather not answer, you can ask for an explanation: "Can you please tell me why you are asking?"

At that point, the interviewer may avoid answering your question and simply move on to the next subject, but he may offer a real and legitimate reason that turns an illegal question into a legal concern and allows you to answer.

If he neither moves on nor rephrases the question, you have no choice but to continue with one of the other approaches, hoping your question has not irrevocably poisoned the atmosphere.

Question the relevance

You can also confront the illegal question with a request that it be explained in the context of the job. If an interviewer asks about your family situation, you may well be wondering what that has to do with your professional competence. Make that concern explicit: "I'm not sure that I understand how my family situation affects my past work or the work I would like to do here, and I'd like to focus on the things that are really important to the job. Can you explain to me how it is relevant to the position we're talking about?"

This is not much different from the previous suggestion, but it does pose a topic that may encourage the interviewer to return to job-specific questions, and it gives her an easy way to get there. An outright refusal to get back to business, however, again leaves you to select one of your other options.

Confront the illegality

Confrontation is never something we hope for in a job interview. We would like everyone to be comfortable. We want the interview to be a conversation between people who find some natural affinity. We want to get along.

It is impossible to predict the interviewer's response if you decide to address illegality directly. Perhaps it was a simple mistake. Perhaps the interviewer doesn't know he crossed the line. Whatever the situation, you can say, "I don't think that's a question you can legally ask in an interview, and I would like to move on to other questions."

Don't expect your interviewer to say, "You're so right, and I don't know what came over me! I've never asked that kind of question before. I apologize, and I'm really impressed with your knowledge of employment law." There is some slight chance that the interviewer knows it was wrong and that he has been legitimately embarrassed by asking the question. There is at least an equal chance that he thinks you are being difficult.

Regardless of the interviewer's response, this is unlikely to be one of your best interviewing moments, at least in terms of the effect it has on your job prospects. If the interviewer drops the question, you have a legitimate reason to feel good about yourself: Some questions are illegal for very good reasons. You have won that battle. Can you still win the war?

You can win if you concentrate your efforts on getting past this awkward situation. It helps if you raised your initial objection in a tactful, matter-of-fact way, not as an aggressive challenge. If you have managed that, and the interviewer does not immediately move on, give him a hand. Change the subject. You can elaborate on something that has gone before: "I wanted to mention something about my role in that marketing project at XYZ Company that I hadn't managed to cover before." You can talk about something that relates to the illegal question, or at least the intent behind it, or you can move on to something completely new.

In any event, regardless of how wrong the interviewer was, it is your job to put things back on course. You may have to swallow your pride, but your willingness to do that depends entirely on how badly you want this job. Only you can decide.

Confront the illegality gently

If you want to bring an illegal question to the interviewer's attention, you can do that gently by noting the illegality and immediately addressing the question that is relevant and legal. Say, for example, that the interviewer has asked about a disability. You know the question is illegal as asked. Your response can call attention to the illegality and move immediately into a more appropriate subject that gives you a chance to demonstrate some positive qualities.

"I am sure that it is illegal for you to ask a question like that, but you may be wondering if I can do the job here. I've spent the last several years in this field, and I took the time to really understand what your company needed before I applied for this job."

After that answer, you can proceed to detail the things you learned and the strengths you would bring to the position. You have showcased your serious approach, and you may even get some points for an answer that shows you are assertive but flexible when dealing with challenging situations.

Drawing the line

A question can be so inappropriate that the interview is beyond all hope of redemption. It may give you such a bad feeling about the company that you are absolutely sure you would never want the job. In that case, it is perfectly appropriate to terminate the interview.

You can walk out the door, with or without telling the interviewer your reasons. You can make it plain that you know the question was illegal, that you can only assume it was a thoughtless mistake, and that you will not dignify it, or any similar question, with an answer. An interview with this kind of unhappy ending is not going to result in a job offer, but it may discourage the interviewer from breaking the law in the future. Future applicants would be grateful—if they only knew.

Be Prepared

Applicants are more likely to be asked illegal and inappropriate questions when they interview with smaller companies. In large companies, HR departments spend much of their time on issues of compliance. They make a point of knowing the regulations that govern hiring practices and treatment of company employees, and they train their staff to apply those laws to their jobs. Big companies know that they leave themselves open to lawsuits if they fail to follow the rules, and they know that their deep pockets make them tempting targets.

Small companies do not have those same resources. Although they may try to stay in compliance with the law, they may not keep up with changes in the regulatory framework, and they often lack separate staff dedicated to the niceties of the hiring process.

Since small-company interviewers are more likely to ask the wrong questions, applicants to those companies should take special note: Before any interview, it pays to prepare as thoroughly as possible. Be prepared for illegal questions, and practice your answers.

With practice, you are less likely to be thrown off guard if you are asked one of those inappropriate questions. Once you have actually given voice to your answers, you are much more likely to arrive at a style of response that feels right to you. The illegal question makes for an uncomfortable moment, and the more naturally you can respond, the more likely it is that you can ease the interview back to more congenial ground. As in any aspect of the interview, the key is to avoid being taken by surprise.

CHAPTER 9

Trick Questions

*We are cups, constantly and quietly being filled.
The trick is, knowing how to tip ourselves
over and let the beautiful stuff out.*

—Ray Bradbury, *Zen in the Art of Writing*

In the best of all possible worlds—or, at least, the best of all possible interviews—every question would be straightforward. Interviewer and applicant would meet on a field of mutual respect and understanding, approaching each other with ultimate sincerity and reaching an exalted state of spiritual communion. Job-search bliss would be attained.

Alas, we have yet to reach that state. At this point in our evolution, interviewees are a suspicious lot, wondering what the interviewer is really getting at with that seemingly innocuous question. Is it a trap? Is she trying to trick me into saying what I shouldn't?

The answer is not likely to redeem one's faith in humanity. In reality, there are questions that qualify as tricks, and the well-prepared applicant should walk into the interview with eyes wide open.

Trick or Treat?

When you're on the hunt for a job, it can become all too easy to think of the interviewer, the HR staff, even the company itself, as the enemy. They're devious. They want to turn you down. In the process, they want to see you squirm.

If you can put those unkind thoughts aside for a moment, it might pay to look at things through the interviewer's eyes. It's something of an understatement to say that the current job market is tough. Companies are greeted by a deluge of candidates for every position, and it's not as if those candidates are uniformly unqualified. In reality, the reverse is true. There are more than enough well-qualified candidates for every position, and the problem for HR departments is weeding out the ones who are less than perfect. Interviewers want to say "yes." In order to get there, they have to say "no" over and over again, and they can't mull over every application at their leisure.

Understandably, they look for shortcuts. Some of those shortcuts are enough to drive an applicant over the edge, such as the use of machines to analyze resumes for keywords, a process that can reject you without the need for time-consuming human intervention. Other shortcuts, such as the use of trick questions, share that same time-saving goal, but they are a double-edged sword. If you prepare for them, you can actually use those trick questions to your advantage.

Make sure, though, that you know what to look for and can avoid the traps the interviewer has laid along the course.

You may find, in the end, that your interviewer is not the Machiavellian schemer you expect, but someone who is asking the very same questions you would ask if you were interviewing yourself.

Look at it another way: Do you have weaknesses? Is there anything in your resume that might raise an interviewer's eyebrow? Are you hoping that you won't be asked about some part of your history? These do not have to be deeply hidden secrets. Sometimes, trick questions are asked in response to something that is right in front of everyone. If you can look at yourself with a moderately objective eye, you can predict what an interviewer will notice. If you prepare, a trick question can be an opportunity rather than a trap.

Behind the Curtain

A list of trick questions could include every interview question ever asked, because any question has the potential to trap an unprepared interviewee. The real tricks, though, have one or more of these characteristics:

- They have a hidden agenda.

- They seem to come out of the blue.

- They seem to invite a particular answer.

- They seem almost too easy.

Note, though, that if the interviewer's agenda is hidden, it is probably hiding in plain sight. As a simple example, consider a question that is asked in many interviews: "Can you describe a situation that gave you trouble at work?"

The interviewer is looking for three things. First, your answer should not consist of a litany of work troubles that outweighs any positive accomplishments of your working life. Second, your answer should not include a work problem that would be a major impediment to your employment. A small problem is more than enough. Third, it is not enough for you to talk about the difficulties you encountered. The "hidden" agenda here is to find out how you handle difficulties, and the important part of your answer describes the way in which you managed the rough spots. You grew. You learned from a mistake.

That agenda is fairly transparent, but it still requires thoughtful answers.

On the Agenda

Although it is impossible to create an exhaustive list of every possible trick question, analyzing a limited selection can be a useful exercise. Sometimes the trick is obvious, but that is not always the case, as these examples demonstrate.

There are some questions whose answers are judged according to their content. What you say actually matters. For other questions, content is less important, and style matters most. In other words, what you say is less important than how you say it.

Did you prepare for this interview?

Sometimes, people are reluctant to admit that they rehearsed. In court cases, for example, it's common for a witness to be asked about preparation, and some witnesses feel that the idea of preparation somehow undercuts the authenticity of their testimony. This is misguided.

People prepare for things that are important to them, such as trials and job interviews. Of course you prepared, but what matters here is what your preparation taught you. Acknowledge that you prepared, and let the interviewer know what you did. You visited the company's website, and you caught up on industry news. You may have spoken to people in the industry.

The more research you show, the more obvious it becomes that this job interview is important to you, and a prospective employer certainly wants to see that. Even better, you can tie what you learned to your reasons for applying to this specific company and to the skills that you will bring to the job. The mistake here is to give a brief answer that doesn't use the question's full potential. This is a real opportunity to sell yourself.

Do you know anyone who works here?

At first glance, this looks like an easy one. Of course you would want to mention any connections that you have at the company—or would you? The answer depends on what you know of that person and how he is perceived by his colleagues. It is always possible that your in-house connection is not very well liked within the company and that your association with him will actually be detrimental. Tread carefully here unless you are comfortable in your knowledge that your contact is a respected employee. Guilt by association, unfair though it may be, is not something to risk.

What things really bother you about coworkers or bosses?

This is not a question that will help interviewees who believe that honesty is the best policy. Everyone has problems with colleagues from time to time, just as they have problems with their spouses, children, parents, and siblings. It's a part of life, but a part of life that has no place in the interview.

Don't take this question as a chance to get critical. Your interviewer wants someone who is positive, not some malcontent who finds fault with everyone within reach. Admittedly, a Pollyanna-like answer is not going to have much credibility, but you can opt for an answer that, for instance, covers the different working styles of your colleagues and describes how you were able to reconcile those styles to create a productive team. With that kind of answer, you avoid excessive negativity and have the opportunity to express something positive.

Why do you want to leave your current job?

As with the previous question, this one could be answered with negatives. You could talk about all the things you hate about your present job, the horrible people, and the Dickensian conditions.

Again, try not to stray into negative territory. A better approach is to turn the table and speak to the things that drew you to the new job. Even better is an answer that ties your motivations to specifics about the company. Focus on the company's strengths, its reputation in the industry, or its way of doing business. You are not leaving your old job because it has become unbearable. You are leaving because of the exciting opportunity in front of you.

What one thing would you change about your current job?

Here is another opportunity to go negative. In fact, the question practically demands it. No job is perfect, so there must be something you would happily change.

If you cannot avoid negativity, at least avoid complaining about people. Demonstrate your desire for the most efficient processes and procedures. Productivity, too. You can mention that despite the smart and talented people at your current job, sloppy systems are stalling the rate of increased sales. You are seeking a position where you'll have a greater opportunity to implement best practices.

What kind of salary do you expect?

This is a topic of perennial debate and not much of a trick, but it is something of a trap. The question raises two issues.

First, it is always better to avoid making the first move. Ideally, you would like the company to put a number on the table and allow you to respond. You can try to postpone the issue, especially if this is a first interview, by saying that you want to focus on the fit between you and the company, and leave questions of compensation until you know that both sides are sincerely interested.

At times, though, this is not an option. In that case, it goes without saying that any number you select should not be astronomical. What is less obvious, perhaps, is that the number should not be unrealistically low. The right answer should be the product of research into industry norms. Try to get a sense of the range offered to people with equivalent experience, similar skills, and comparable education to you. Narrow that range by considering company size and location, since those factors make a difference. You can be comfortable offering a number at the top of that range, but you have to know that range before you put a number on the table.

How did you manage to make time for this interview?

This question is directed at people who are already employed, and the interviewer is really asking about your tendency to use company time for other pursuits.

This is another moment to avoid baring your soul. You may have taken personal time. You typically schedule interviews after hours and would insist on that if possible. You only meet with matches that are close to perfection. Do not give the interviewer the sense that you are abusing your present employer's time. Make it clear that you are sensitive to the issue. You would never give less than a day's work for a day's pay.

Where do you see yourself in five years?

This question appears again and again. Its trickiness lies only in the fact that the interviewer wants to know, perhaps among other things, that you plan to be with the company for a substantial time if you are hired. You can say a lot about your interest in improving your skills, educating yourself further, and making increasing contributions in your work. Whatever you decide to say, you want to say that all of those things should be happening at a great company where you can make a difference by utilizing your expertise. For extra credit, tie your vision of your future self to specifics about the company's operations.

If you won the lottery, would you still work?

At the risk of belaboring the point, honesty is not necessarily your friend in an interview. Your true answer may be that you would quit immediately and never look back. A better option is to focus on the value of work. Work is a meaningful part of your life, not just a way to pay the bills, and you cannot imagine leaving it behind completely.

If you can, try to keep a straight face when delivering your answer.

What would your ideal job be like?

True or not, for the purposes of the interview, your ideal job looks very much like the one you are applying for at this very company.

This is another situation in which it helps to know a lot about the company. That knowledge can be the basis for your description of an ideal job that is attainable in the current context, even if it is not exactly the job in question today.

The question might be phrased differently: "Where would you really like to work?" The answer should still focus on the virtues of the current position. It should also reiterate your desire to work for an excellent company where you can apply your skills and experience.

The Outer Limits

Some questions may not qualify as tricks, but they deserve mention along with the tricks because they are out of the ordinary, at times extremely so. Interview surprises are rarely fun.

Some of these questions fall into the puzzle category. In some interviews, especially for jobs in technology, a candidate may be asked to solve a problem or demonstrate a skill. In those cases, problems and skills are related to the applicant's field of work.

Another type of question, however, bears no obvious relation to a particular job.

Those questions are the ones favored by companies such as Google and Microsoft. The most famous example is the question that asks why manhole covers are round.

There is no real trick involved. The essence of the question is the process, so the quality of the answer matters less than the quality of the applicant's problem-solving ability. Let the interviewer know what you are thinking, and never give an answer without a coherent explanation.

There are also interviewers who decide that a touch of whimsy is what the interview needs. If you were an animal, what kind of animal would you be? What kind of tree? Who is your favorite Muppet?

No one can tell you how to answer those off-the-wall questions, except to say that your selection should reflect the qualities that are desirable in the job, and that how you get to an answer is more important than the actual identity of your favorite Muppet. Some interviewers throw out these kinds of questions to see how easily flustered you are. Now, at least, you can go into an interview with an awareness that questions can come out of left field.

There are, in fact, questions whose primary purpose is to put the interviewee on the spot—for instance, "What would you say if I told you that this interview is going terribly?"

One option, of course, is to take the remark very personally and respond with a great wailing and gnashing of teeth, but this is not optimal. A far better approach is to stop, take a deep breath, and think before answering. What is the interviewer getting at? Is she trying to make me angry or upset? Perhaps she is, and you can calmly tell her that you would be upset if she was correct. The job is very important to you, you prepared in depth, and you want to join this company very much. You would be terribly disappointed. You might ask where she thinks it all went wrong. The last thing you want to do is lose your cool.

With every question, that's good advice to heed. Think before you answer. Try to turn things to your advantage when you can. Focus on the positives, and remind yourself that you didn't get here by accident. Your competition is just as human as you are.

If you can remain poised in this very stressful situation, an interviewer's bag of tricks need hardly be a threat at all.

CHAPTER 10

Say "Thank You" and Mean It

Always do right. This will gratify some
people and astonish the rest.

—Mark Twain

After a job interview is over, many job seekers think the ball is in the prospective employer's court. After all, you've made your case to be hired and put your best foot forward. What more is there to do except wait for a decision?

Actually, something as simple as writing a thank-you letter can go a long way toward tipping the scales in your favor. Here are just a few of the reasons why you might want to take a minute or two out of your job hunt to write one:

- It says a lot about you. By not sending a thank-you letter, you can give the impression that you lack initiative and follow-through, and if the employer is debating between you and another equally qualified candidate who did send a thank-you, guess who will get the job?

- It helps you stand out. Recruiters interview a lot of candidates for each open position at a company, and while they may fully intend to give due consideration to each applicant, they are only human. Their memories may get fuzzy after a long day of interviews. By recapping some of the points you made in the interview in your thank-you letter, you get another chance to remind them of your strengths.

- It gives you a second chance. Who hasn't left a job interview and thought of a better answer to a question that was posed to them? While you can't actually go back and do the interview again, you can use your thank-you letter as a way to make sure your better answer gets heard by the people you're trying to impress.

- It could force a reply. Sure, they said they'd let you know in a few days, but they haven't gotten back to you. It could mean they're not interested, or it could mean they're just dragging their feet. If it's the latter, getting correspondence from you might remind them that they still have a decision to make, and you might well be the beneficiary of a second interview as a result. In any job market, making sure you set yourself apart after the interview may be the critical factor in securing your new position within a company. Therefore, it's essential to be sure that you follow up after the interview.

Too many people who are interviewing for a position don't take the time to follow up. They worry that the hiring managers and others involved in the interview are too busy, or that following up with a thank-you note or letter will seem too desperate. If an applicant believes that the interview went awry or that the job isn't what it seemed, he may feel that a follow-up isn't necessary.

No matter how you feel about the interview, the interviewers, or the company, remember this: following up with a letter will show your enthusiasm and ability to follow through, and it will provide you with one last opportunity to make your case for why you should be hired.

So, what can you do to make sure that your follow-up hits its mark?

First, you'll want to look at the follow-up as a part of your job-search strategy. Recognize the thank-you letter as the valuable tool that it is. Though your focus should be on the interview itself, make sure that at the end of the interview, you're leaving with the information you need. Take notes during the interview that you can reference in your thank-you note. Ask questions about the hiring process and when you might hear something, but also take the time to collect the names and titles of all of the individuals who took part in the interview. Additionally, make sure that you learn the best way to contact those individuals after the interview.

Whether the preferred method of contact is email or postal mail, you will want to be sure to craft a timely note to thank your interviewers. By sending an individual thank-you card or letter to each person within 24 hours of the interview, you will be able to show your appreciation for their time, make a final statement as to why you're the best candidate for the position, and provide any additional information that may have been requested. If there were any details that you left out during the interview, a follow-up note is another opportunity to share them.

Before you send your thank-you notes or letters—whether they are handwritten, typed, or sent via email—proofread them for grammar and spelling. If you express intentions to follow up by phone, be sure to schedule such calls in your calendar prior to sending the notes.

By taking the time to ask about when a hiring decision will be made, following up after the interview with a thank-you letter, and being patient but persistent, you will show your commitment. You will also showcase your ability to follow directions, continue to demonstrate your interest, and begin to form relationships with those at the company.

Being proactive and showing initiative—without over-doing it, of course—by following up after the interview demonstrates your professionalism. More importantly, the right follow-up is an opportunity to set yourself apart from others who have applied for the position you want to call your own.

A Very Brief History of the Job Interview: The Modern Era

The change wrought by the Industrial Revolution at the beginning of the 19th century was not something that improved conditions immediately for all. On one hand, the factories needed workers, and people wanted jobs. They migrated to the cities for jobs that paid better than farm laboring; and the jobs were, indeed, waiting for them. On the other hand, this was the era of the seven-day workweek, of child labor, and of the prohibition of unions. Work may not have been hard to come by, but working conditions could be difficult to survive.

As time went by, working conditions improved. But even in 1900, employers could be heard muttering a familiar complaint: The workers were not all they could be. They lacked knowledge and skills. They were a rather disappointing lot.

One man who shared this view was Thomas Edison, a man who could serve as an embodiment of the Industrial Revolution. He was churning out inventions, but he had a problem. His employees, though college educated, were not living up to the standards he set. In other words, they did not know as much as Edison himself did.

If Edison could not count on the mere possession of a college degree to guarantee that an employee met his standards, he needed another way to decide among applicants. To that end, he devised what many have called the first modern job interview, a test consisting of 150 questions, some tailored to the specific role the applicant hoped to fill, others asked of everyone.

As part of its Edison National Historical Park website, the National Park Service lets you put yourself in the shoes of one of Edison's applicants and answer the questions yourself. It advises you to think as if you are taking the test in 1921. Among the general questions:

- What countries border France?

- Where is the Volga River?

- What country grows the finest cotton?

- Before World War I, what country drank the most tea?

- What U.S. city leads the nation in manufacturing laundry machines?

- What city is the U.S. fur center?

- Which is bigger, Australia or Greenland?

- What is the largest telescope in the world?

- Who was Paul Revere?

- Who was Danton?

- Who was Solon?

- Where is Labrador?

- How did America get its name?

- Where was Columbus born?

- What is a dinosaur?

- What do white corpuscles do?

If you were a specialist, you might be asked something different. Edison asked cabinetmakers what country mahogany came from and, perhaps having a certain carpenter in mind, the identity of the emperor of Rome at the time of Christ's birth. Logically enough, masons had to compute the cubic yards of concrete in a wall of a certain size, but they were also asked to name

Lincoln's assassin, a question that bears no obvious relation to the mason's trade.

The test was something of a sensation in its day, and, just as today's Google and Microsoft questions are badly kept secrets, the Edison test found its way into newspapers after test takers leaked the questions. As a result, Edison had to repeatedly revise his questionnaire.

An applicant had to score at least 90 percent to pass the test. Of 718 test takers, only 10 percent received passing grades. What did it mean? It meant something to its creator, at least. "Only 2 percent of the people think, as I gather from my questionnaire," Edison said.

The real question, though, was whether the test was a good tool for its purpose. Apparently, Edison's son Theodore, then a student at MIT, couldn't manage a passing grade. Albert Einstein, according to the National Park Service, was another failure. Today, the use of the test is explained by Edison's need for well-rounded collaborators, not narrow specialists, and by the supposition that the test was a mirror of Edison's own eclectic mind.

The 150-question Edison test became famous, but it was not the first test that Edison devised for prospective employees. In 1883, for example, he had 92 questions that were asked of central station engineers, who helped bring electricity into broad commercial use for the first time. Those questions were highly technical and quite specific—for instance, "How much zinc is removed and deposited in one minute by an ampere of current?" For those questions, he solicited input from various associates, his "boys," and asked them to provide as many different answers as possible before subjecting outsiders to the test. This kind of examination is almost exactly analogous to today's interviews that require applicants to demonstrate an actual job-specific knowledge or skill.

Although he did not leave us much evidence of his motives, Edison must have felt that the new, more general test told him something that the technical test did not. Perhaps the test made sense because a job with Edison required a great deal of collaboration and a multidisciplinary approach. He was looking for employees who could see beyond a particular technical specialty. The broad range of Edison's many inventions seems to give that explanation some credibility.

Edison's test was enough of a phenomenon to inspire imitators, and other businesses followed in the great man's footsteps, just as companies today follow the lead of successful organizations.

CHAPTER 11

The New Interview, Courtesy of Google and Others

Strength of mind is exercise, not rest.
—Alexander Pope, *An Essay on Man*

The job interview has been part of the hiring process for as long as anyone looking for a job can remember. It has evolved over the years, to be sure, and some of the changes are easy to see. Today's interviews have adopted the behavioral approach, which asks applicants to report specific occasions on which they had to rely on critical core competencies. The process is, as it has been for many years, an attempt to tie the artifice of the interview to the reality of working life, but it is not clear that the behavioral approach is an actual improvement over earlier interview techniques.

The problem for interviewers is that every innovation is quickly publicized, especially in our hyper-connected online world. Applicants get the word on the latest questions. They rehearse their interview performances. They think of representative situations for every possible strength or weakness.

The elephant in the interview room is the glaring uncertainty of whether an interview can be relied on to do the one thing it sets out to do: Find the best candidate for the position.

The ability of the interview to do that has been studied over the years, and those studies have found that some general principles seem to improve the process, at least from the employer's standpoint. Panel interviews tend to yield more reliability among interviewers in terms of their grading of different candidates. Structured interviews, in which all candidates are asked the same questions, tend to be more reliable than unstructured interviews. Behavioral interviews, which by their nature fall within a more structured framework, are more useful than psychological interviews, which are intended to evaluate broad personal qualities such as dependability and conscientiousness.

Even when interviewers limit their tactics to those most likely to give good results, the correlation between interview performance and job performance is far from perfect. In one meta-analysis of previous research, structured interviews won out over unstructured ones, but the distinction was far from dramatic, according to a 1994 paper published in the *Journal of Applied Psychology*.[1] That paper went on to add a host of caveats to any conclusions we might be tempted to draw.

The bad news for the interviewer, then, is that there is no truly definitive way to make sure the interview process results in finding the right candidate for the job. There are those in the interviewing trade for whom this is all a bit much. Moved, perhaps, by the futility of their task, they opted for off-the-wall questions. "If you were a tree, what kind of tree would you be?"

At the same time, some companies were taking their own idiosyncratic approaches to the hiring process, with Google being a prime example. It asked candidates to demonstrate—on the spot—skills that would apply to particular jobs. When Google didn't do that, it posed hypothetical problems for candidates to solve, some more like riddles or brainteasers than typical interview questions.

Google was not the first or the only company to depart from the standard interview process, but its route to that departure is especially relevant in today's economy.

Google's hiring staff, even in good economic times, faced an unusual problem: an embarrassment of riches. Almost from the beginning, it had more applicants than it could possibly employ, and they were lining up for jobs of their own accord.

In recent years, with the job market at its worst in decades, every company has been a potential Google. Yes, they recruit, but they can afford to be very picky, and the Google style of interview question had become more and more popular.

What is Google Thinking?

What kinds of brainteasers fall into the Google-question category? What can an applicant do to prepare? Are there some questions that are asked again and again? Is there a theme?

What is the point, anyway?

The point, obviously, is to hire the best people. That means, though, hiring the best people as Google defines that term. Those may not be the best people for another company. They may not even be the people who would have shined at Google 10 years ago.

They have some identifiable characteristics: They're smart. They solve problems. They think through those problems to find creative solutions. They are pragmatic, in a sense, because they are able to approach problems with open minds. They brainstorm. They can follow the consequences of their ideas. They are adaptable and can revise their approaches as conditions change. They do not discard the simple solution in favor of complexity if the simple solution works. They pay attention to the terms of a problem, instead of making assumptions.

That's a pretty intimidating list of qualities, and it's asking a lot for any interview question to reveal that much about the candidate.

Google uses two different approaches to make the process work.

The first is directed at technical candidates such as software engineers. It is an actual test, not a question about the meaning of life or the best way to handle some bizarre hypothetical situation. Google wants to see applicants work. To that end, an in-person interviewee is confronted with a whiteboard, and an online interview is frequently conducted through Google Docs. In the latter case, the interviewer is watching the applicant work as she types.

Asked to code their way to a solution, and with someone looking over their shoulders, candidates had better know their stuff and be able to walk the interviewer through the problem. They are always showing their work as they go.

If the interview is face-to-face, the applicant's code is likely to be put to the test on the spot. The interviewer may be sitting with a laptop, typing in the very code the applicant is writing on the whiteboard. It leaves little room for code that won't run, and it tests applicants' skills in the most immediate way imaginable, pressure cooker included.

The coding assignments themselves are hardly unusual, but they can be difficult, especially in such a stressful environment. Some examples are:

- Design a calendar system that accounts for meeting times and attendees; give it the ability to sort according to any of a number of criteria; and be sure it can highlight overlapping schedules.

- Design a system that efficiently allocates cell phone numbers.

- Given an array, find the maximum consecutive sum of its integers.

- Design an algorithm to catalog all of the books in the world.

- Write an algorithm that will make change for any amount of U.S. coins.

It's hard to say that these coding exercises are unfair—applicants are being asked to do something that is completely related to their jobs—but Google does not make life easy for them. There is pressure inherent in the situation, no matter how the interviewer behaves, and Google turns up the heat a bit and takes things a step further. Interviewers at Google are, famously, a poker-faced lot. If you ever have an interview at Google, don't expect encouragement or positive feedback. In fact, don't expect much feedback at all. No one will be complimenting you on the good job you're doing.

That approach seems designed to remove some of the human element from the process, perhaps hoping to create a more objective evaluation. The Google interview is definitely not about hitting it off with the interviewer, although that doesn't hurt. Instead, it's all about getting down to business and hitting it off with that whiteboard or keyboard.

The second Google approach is the one that has become so well known that other companies have borrowed it. It is applied to candidates for almost every position at Google, and it's here that interviewers break out the riddles, bizarre hypotheticals, and logic puzzles. The interviewee is still greeted by a blank face across the desk, but this is no longer about answers that are right or wrong. Instead, we are talking about answers that are good or better or more interesting, and the way an applicant reaches those answers is at least as important as the answers themselves.

A Brief History of the Job Interview: Introducing Science and Structure

There was plenty of structure in Thomas Edison's famous 150-question test for prospective employees, but it does not seem that he ever studied its reliability as a predictor of workplace success. Perhaps he was right, and the test proved that "only 2 percent of the people think," but we are forced to take his conclusion on faith.

Sometimes it takes a crisis to get people to look closely at accepted practices. In the United States, that crisis came with World War II, when winning the war in the air was crucial and pilots were scarce. The training of pilots was an expensive business, and too many of the men being trained did not make it to the end of the course. In 1941, John C. Flanagan, a psychologist, joined the United States Army Air Forces (USAAF) and, together with 150 other psychologists and some 1,400 assistants, set about improving the selection process.

Flanagan ultimately developed the method he called the critical incident technique, or CIT, a cornerstone of USAAF's Aviation Psychology Program. The essence of CIT lies in "gathering certain important facts concerning behavior in defined situations."[2] It requires an understanding of the purpose of a given activity performed in a particular situation, followed by an analysis of what behaviors are critical to the successful performance of that activity. Once those parameters are defined, it becomes possible to analyze the relationship between behavior in one situation, such as a training exercise, and behavior in another situation, generally where an activity has to be performed for real.

The way the pilots behaved offered a good indication of how they would respond if faced with the same situation in real life.

Using the technique, one of Flanagan's colleagues, S. C. Ericksen, was able to develop an objective proficiency test for civilian pilots of light aircraft, a test that would identify pilots likely to succeed in the military.

A similar project examined the standard flight check. Trainee pilots were presented with "situations providing uniformly standard opportunities to perform critical aspects of the airline pilot's job."[3] Using that approach, agreement among different examiners increased to 88 percent from a level that had been little better than chance.

According to another of Flanagan's colleagues, William Clemans, CIT produced pilots who were "virtually assured of success."[4]

For the military at that time, a test or technique that was reliable, in that different examiners reached the same conclusions, and valid, in that it predicted future performance with some accuracy, was the answer to a prayer. Today, hiring managers share that same agenda.

Once Flanagan's approach became known, corporations leaped to adopt the principles espoused by Flanagan, just as they had embraced Edison's methods. They liked the idea that there were critical abilities that were prerequisites to superior job performance, and they liked the idea that there was a legitimate way to identify and test for those abilities. Admittedly, criteria for success in the corporate world are not always as clear as they were in the world of combat flight, but Flanagan's techniques introduced a focus on critical behaviors as opposed to vaguely defined character traits.

In time, that new focus led to the structured interview, a style that is now almost ubiquitous. Instead of being asked to elaborate on his strengths and weaknesses, a candidate is presented with behavioral or situational questions. In a well-designed interview, those questions will elicit responses that actually have some bearing on the critical skills needed on the job.

The only difference between behavioral and situational questions is their time frame. Behavioral questions ask about past behavior. Situational questions ask about hypothetical situations that an employee might face in the future. Situational questions have the advantage of allowing interviewers to delve into critical areas, even if the candidate has no experience in those areas.

The real lesson of Flanagan's CIT, though, is that the emphasis should be on the questions, not the answers. The technological equivalent is GIGO (garbage-in, garbage-out), which means that you cannot expect worthwhile output if you do not supply meaningful input. The challenge for the interviewer is finding the questions that stand a chance of eliciting meaningful responses in context.

Once you acknowledge that the interview is all about the questions, it's a fairly short step to the questions famously asked in today's Google interview. At first glance, they are almost non sequiturs. The question seems to have nothing to do with the job.

One such question from Google is a situational hypothetical: You have been reduced to the size of a nickel and dropped in a blender. The blades will start turning in one minute. What do you do?

We can hope that this is one situation you won't actually encounter at Google, but the far-fetched nature of the hypothetical underscores the importance of the question relative to its answer. A response such as "pray for deliverance" won't earn many points, but there really is no right or wrong answer. Instead of focusing on your answer's rightness or wrongness, the interviewer wants to know how you think about a challenging problem. How do you analyze the situation? What questions do you ask? How do you think things through? In this interview, the critical skill at issue is your problem-solving ability.

In both concept and execution, the interview has changed dramatically over the years.

In its earliest days, the very idea of asking questions could elicit a hostile response, at least from a terribly sensitive artist.

Today, to the contrary, the very idea of a job application without an interview is almost incomprehensible. What kind of employer doesn't want to talk to you?

Whether your interview is a trial by fire or a pleasant conversation, however, two things have become clear after more than 250 years of interview history:

the success of an interview depends at least as much on the interviewer as the interviewee; and the entire process, for all its evolution, is still more art than science.

When the Going Gets Weird

What kind of bizarre questions might an applicant face, then?

Before launching into a list of possibilities, it makes sense to gain a bit of perspective.

First, no list will be exhaustive. The universe of questions is simply too large. Second, no list will be accurate. Google is not foolish enough to repeat the same questions ad infinitum, and, to make matters more difficult, Google is not interested in having its interviewing techniques broadcast. For the latter reason, many Google interviews are governed by nondisclosure agreements signed by the candidates, and many candidates take those agreements seriously.

Are those objections enough to make the exercise useless? No, because even if you don't know the exact questions you will be asked at a Google interview, you gain a lot from understanding the style of questions that is typical.

Finally, even if you're not interested in applying for a job at Google, hiring, like almost every aspect of business, has its fashions. Companies copy each other. Companies that are successful are copied most of all. Google is an extremely successful company.

Employers copy Google, and these are the kinds of questions that, rightly or wrongly, hiring managers have come to associate with the presumably superior practices of successful companies. Managers, thinking that Google must know what it's doing, are all too willing to jump on the weird-question bandwagon.

As a result, smart applicants will want to know what might be in store, even if that means devoting some time to considering questions that seem ridiculously irrelevant.

One question that you are unlikely to hear is generally attributed to Microsoft: Why are manhole covers round? It's the best known of the oddball questions. For that reason alone, you will hear it only from an interviewer who is an amateur, someone who came across the manhole question somewhere and thought it might be fun to ask. Do not expect to hear it from a big company with professional hiring staff. However, there is no shortage of unconventional replacements for the manhole cover.

Numbers

Some questions posit a seemingly simple problem, generally something numerical, and ask for a solution. For example:

- How many golf balls does it take to fill a school bus?

- How many dogs are there in the world?

- How many manhole covers—yes, those again—are there in New York City?

- How many houses are painted red in Seattle?

- How many people are on their cell phones right now in Boston?

No one expects you to know the answers to questions like these. The interviewer is equally clueless. The point of the question is not for you to reach the "right" answer. In fact, the point is for you to demonstrate the thought process you apply to a problem when the answer is unknown from the beginning. The theory behind the exercise is that you use that same thought process for every project on the job.

Stories
Some questions start as little stories. They offer a premise, and they generally ask you to find a way to do something within the bounds set by that premise. These questions call for logical reasoning. Here, too, numbers often make an appearance. Some questions tell simple stories, but others get more elaborate. Here are some examples:

- You are driving a car with a helium balloon tied to the floor. What happens to the balloon when you accelerate?

- You live in a society in which all parents want a boy and couples keep having children until they have a boy. What is the proportion of boys to girls in your society?

- You have a bag of 10 coins, nine of which are of the same weight. One weighs less than the others. Given a balance scale and three chances to weigh any number of coins, how can you determine which coin weighs less? What if you didn't know that one coin weighed less but only that one coin was different?

- You are a pirate captain who needs to split a large treasure among your crew. Everyone gets to vote on your proposed split, but you'll end up walking the plank if you don't get at least half of all the pirates to agree with your proposal. What do you propose?

- You're at a party with Bob and Eve. You want to know if Bob has your correct phone number without asking him directly. You can, however, write something on a card and have Eve deliver the card. You do not want to disclose your phone number to Eve. What can you write on the card?

Whether or not you immediately leap to the correct answers, there are lessons to be learned from these questions.

For the helium balloon, the interviewee should realize that the question would not be asked unless there was something odd about the situation. Why wouldn't a helium balloon act like everything around it? What's the catch? You might ask yourself what sets a helium balloon apart from other things inside the car. What is it about helium that's noteworthy?

Helium balloons, unlike their air-filled counterparts, rise.

As it turns out, a helium balloon behaves differently from, say, a person in that same car because of the very quality that makes it float up into the sky: it's less dense. It will behave like an air bubble in a carpenter's level. That air bubble, because it is less dense, acts independently of the fluid in which it sits. You may not get to that answer, but it's the thought process that counts, starting with the recognition that there is something worth noticing about the problem. Your goal is to spot the "catch." Without that ability, you can only guess at answers.

The phone number problem illustrates something different. It's a tough one for programmers, in particular, because it calls up notions of security and encrypted communications.

Indeed, there are answers that get pretty sophisticated, but they may not get full marks. What was the question, again? You want to know if Bob has your correct phone number. Perhaps you could ask him to give you a call. If your phone rings, you have your answer. That keeps Eve out of the loop, doesn't it?

It's a pretty simple solution that underlines the importance of listening to the question that is actually being asked. Listen. Don't leap to conclusions. Don't go for complexity when something simple works best, and this question was all too simple.

That approach is also illustrated by another interview question: How would you make a million dollars in a day if you had 10,000 Apache servers at your disposal? You should not leap at a sophisticated answer unless you are convinced that you could not reach your goal by simply selling the lot of them.

Products and design

A third category of questions asks that you design something. It can be built from scratch or it can be an improvement to an existing product. Interviewees may be given challenges such as these:

- Design a classroom.

- Design a shopping center.

- Design an evacuation plan for San Francisco.

- How would you improve Gmail?

- How would you improve your favorite website?

- Design a windshield wiper that is an improvement over current wipers.

- How would you go about monetizing Google Chrome?

Google interviewers tend to ask these kinds of questions about Google products. Other companies ask about their own products. The important point is that if you claim to be an ardent user of Gmail, for example, make sure you know Gmail inside and out. You do not want to follow in the footsteps of candidates—and such candidates apparently exist—who suggested improvements that were already incorporated into the service.

The fact that you may be asked questions like these makes it all the more important that you research the company with which you are interviewing. Know something about its products, the challenges it faces, its goals, and its position in the industry. The more you know, the better your chance of impressing your interviewer.

Google Gives Advice

Google is happy to provide some advice to people it interviews, and the advice is simple and to the point.

According to the book *Are You Smart Enough to Work at Google?*, here are Google's own tips:

- It's ok to question your interviewer.

- When asked to provide a solution, first define and framework the problem as you see it.

- If you don't understand—ask for help or clarification.

- If you need to assume something—verbally check it's a correct assumption!

- Describe how you want to tackle solving each part of the question.

- Always let your interviewer know what you are thinking, as he/she will be as interested in your process of thought as your solution. Also, if you're stuck, they may provide hints if they know what you're doing.

- Finally, listen—don't miss a hint if your interviewer is trying to assist you.[5]

Those tips can be applied to challenging interview questions at any company, although it's not clear that Google interviewers spend much of their time "trying to assist you."

Often, it's more of a trial by fire, especially for the more technical positions. That is nothing new for Google, and where Google goes, others follow.

Whether any of this works at helping hirers to select the right candidate is another question, but you can see the roots of the approach in an early Google experience that has become something of an old chestnut.

For the first five years of Google's existence, founders Larry Page and Sergey Brin did all of their own interviewing. Alissa Lee, a lawyer, was one of those interviewed. Brin gave her a task. He asked her to draft a contract and email it to him within 30 minutes. The contract was to cover the sale of Brin's soul to the devil.

According to Ken Auletta's *Googled: The End of the World as We Know It*, Lee forgot to ask the questions she should have asked, but she got the job, and she now thinks those questions were beside the point. To Lee, what moved Brin was that "he was looking for someone who could embrace a curveball, even relish it, and thrive in the process of tackling something unexpected."[6] We may never know much about the quality of the contract Lee drafted, but her attitude was what made a difference.

Lee's task, of course, had something of a direct relationship to her job, and that relationship is far from clear for many of today's challenging questions. Even if you think that the current fashion for off-the-wall questions and peculiar puzzles is completely misguided—and there are many who share that opinion—the fashion is firmly entrenched in the interview rooms of corporate America.

Asking challenging questions may be no better than asking for a description of your strengths and weaknesses, but those challenging questions are here to stay, and they have spread to all levels of business. Whether you are interviewing at Google or at a small local business, be prepared.

CHAPTER 12

Turn the Tables: When It's Your Turn to Pose Questions

I'll just take charge of the pistol for a while.
—Fritz Robinson in the film *Swiss Family Robinson*, directed by Ken Annakin

An interview is not a place to wing it.

Most people understand this, and few job applicants are so confident that they plan to improvise their answers to interview questions. Most people prepare, and they find abundant resources to help them.

Prepare, by all means. Make a list of questions, and answer them out loud. Enlist a friend to play the interviewer's part. Polish your delivery. Solicit feedback.

So far, so good—but you are far from ready for the main event. In fact, you're only halfway there, because you have looked at only one side of the interview coin.

Regardless of the job or the company, the essence of the interview scenario is always the same: You've answered all the questions. Perhaps you feel good about your answers, or at least you feel that you haven't embarrassed yourself. The interview seems to be winding down.

Before you rise for a valedictory handshake, though, there is always one more bridge to cross. It comes when the interviewer looks across the table and asks, "Do you have any questions?"

The importance of this moment cannot be overemphasized. It is your single best opportunity to shine. It is your best chance to show that you are here for all the right reasons. Given this opening, you can prove that you have the intelligence, interest, and engagement that any employer wants to see in a prospective hire.

To understand the importance of the moment, remember that a job interview differs in important ways from most social interactions. The interviewer expects you to behave in certain highly structured ways. Unlike an everyday conversation, this interaction has a particular goal. Put most simply, the interviewer is looking for someone who can solve the company's problems, whatever they may be. Whether you are interviewing for the top job or for the position of assistant to an assistant's assistant, you have to convince someone you have just met that you are right for the job and are a cut above any other candidates.

You can make a powerful case for yourself by asking the right questions, because your questions let you show the interviewer something important about your potential at the company. Your answers to the interviewer's questions matter, of course, but your questions can matter even more.

First, an interaction has to be a two-way street for participants to feel good about it. We may not be able to quantify "feeling good," but that does not make it a trivial concern. If we can assume that you and your interviewer are both human, human nature is going to play its part in your interaction. If you both feel good at the end of the interview, that is one sign you have done your job, but no one feels good about a conversation in which one person does all the talking. A one-sided conversation is not something that satisfies us as human beings. In fact, it's not even a conversation. A job interview is not exempt from these fundamental considerations.

Second, the questions you ask can tell the interviewer something important about you. They let you demonstrate that you have done your homework about the company and the job. You haven't picked this employer out of a hat. You know what the company does and how it does it. You understand its goals. You know how the company and its industry have changed over the years. You know how the company fits into that industry. The fact that you have taken the trouble to learn all this is something that can forcefully distinguish your application from those of the competition, and there is no better way to illustrate that fact than by asking the right questions. They may well be the questions the company asks itself.

Third, your questions also tell the interviewer what kind of employee you will be. Are you seriously thinking ahead to what you can contribute once you're hired? Have you thought through how your skills meet the company's needs? By asking the right questions, you lead your interviewer to the best answers to his own questions.

Finally, consider a more subtle purpose of your questions. Everything you do is meant to influence your interviewer, consciously or unconsciously, in one very specific direction: you deserve to be hired. Not all of your influence comes from the content of the things you say. Instead, much of it comes from the way in which you say things. How you frame your own interview questions can push your interviewer, even unconsciously, to see you as a serious candidate. You see yourself as a serious candidate. You want your interviewer to agree, to picture you in the job, and to feel satisfied with that picture.

Clearly, then, asking good questions is more than filling dead air. Your questions show that you're here for a reason. Yes, everyone is here to get a job, just like you, but you have something extra. You are not here to get just any job. You are here to get this job, at this time, in this place, in this field, with this particular company.

Traditionally, interview preparation has tended to focus on answering the questions you expect to hear, but that approach ends up missing a golden opportunity. Spend a good chunk of your preparation time compiling your own questions. Add them to your arsenal so you can turn a stiff, formal, and artificial examination into a productive conversation.

Choosing the Questions to Ask

To get started, here are some examples. Remember that some of your questions—in fact, some of your best questions—will be specific to the company and job for which you are interviewing. Those questions must be customized, but the following examples can serve as jumping-off points for you to craft your own approach.

General questions

Note that these are questions about the company and the job, but they are not questions about how you will benefit from being hired, except when that benefit applies to ways in which you can learn and improve on the job. In other words, the focus is on *your commitment to benefit the company.* Even questions about advancement within the company can have an underlying assumption that you expect to do the kind of work that merits advancement.

- How long has this position been open?

- Is this a new position? If so, why was it created? If not, why did the person who held this position leave the position?

- What are the company's priorities, and what specific results would be expected from me in the first 90 days or so?

- What kinds of opportunities for advancement are available?

- Why did you join the company? How long ago was that? What is it about the company that keeps you here?

- Did my resume raise any questions I can clarify?

- What do you look for in an employee?

- What type of training is required? What does it consist of, and how long is it? Beyond any required training, what other types of training are available?

- What would my first assignment be?

- What are the skills and attributes most needed to get ahead here?

- How regularly do performance evaluations occur?

- Do you have a job description available for this position?

- Are there any expansion plans for the company?

- What are the opportunities for on-the-job training and further education?

- Do you have a tuition assistance or book reimbursement program?

- How would you evaluate the company's position compared to industry competitors' positions?

- What kind of follow-up from me would be most useful to you?

Questions for headhunters and recruiters

As most applicants know, the recruitment process doesn't always begin with direct contact with the company. If you are going through an intermediary, such as a recruiter, you may not be able to elicit company-specific answers. You may also want to clarify the hiring procedure and the recruiter's relationship with the company she represents. Try to get specific information about the person on the other side of the relationship, as recruiters may not volunteer much about their clients beyond the basics.

In this situation, you are dealing with a sort of gate-keeper, and your goal is to move past this round so that the real work of getting hired can begin. With recruiters who provide little information about their clients, you are in no position to demonstrate your familiarity with the hiring company, but that allows some interview leeway. You can be a bit more self-centered in this situation.

- Are you dealing with the client's HR people, or do you have direct contact with the hiring manager?

- How many candidates have you placed with this client? How long have you worked with this client?

- Have you placed other candidates in similar positions with this client? If not, what other sorts of positions have you placed candidates in with this client?

- May I have a written job description?

- Where is the position located?

- To whom does the position report?

- Is this a new position? If not, why is the position open?

- What happened to the person who previously held this position?

- How long have you been working on the assignment?

- What does the position pay?

- Are there any pay or compensation constraints that I should take into consideration?

- What can you tell me about the person who will be interviewing me? What is his or her position, title, management style?

- Who will make the final hiring decision?

- After you present my resume, when can I expect to hear from you regarding the status of this position?

- If your client is interested, will my next contact be directly with the company?

- If your client has questions or needs additional information, will they contact me or will they continue working through your office?

Questions to ask HR

When dealing with an HR department, especially in a large company, you may not be able to get the specific answers you would expect from someone working in the department you want to join. In that case, the interview gives you the chance to improve your sense of what life is like for a current employee.

- Why do you enjoy working for this company?

- What attracted you to this organization?

- Can you describe the work environment here?

- How do you describe the philosophy of the organization?

- What do you consider to be the organization's strengths and weaknesses?

- Can you tell me more about my day-to-day responsibilities?

- How soon are you looking to fill this position?

- I have really enjoyed meeting with you and your team, and I am very interested in the opportunity. I feel my skills and experience would be a good match for this position. What is the next step in your interview process?

- Before I leave, is there anything else you need to know concerning my ability to do this job?

- In your opinion, what is the most important contribution that this company expects from its employees?

- If I'm hired, what will constitute success during my first six months on the job?

- I know the company decided to recruit from outside the organization for this position. How do you decide between recruiting from within and going outside?

- What advice would you give to someone in my position?

- What major problems are we facing right now in this department or position?

- Can you give me a formal, written description of the position? I'm interested in reviewing in detail the major activities involved and what results are expected.

- Can you please tell me a little bit about the people with whom I'll be working most closely?

Questions to ask hiring managers

If your interviewer is a hiring manager, the line of questioning may not play to your strengths. With a few simple questions, you can plot a course that is more likely to advance your interests.

- What specific skills would a new hire bring that would make your life easier?

- What are some of the challenges on the job that keep you up at night?

- What are some of the skills and abilities you see as necessary for someone to succeed in this job?

- What would be a surprising but positive thing the new person could do in the first 90 days?

- What challenges might I encounter if I take on this position?

- Will we be expanding or bringing on new products or new services that I should be aware of?

- What major concerns need to be immediately addressed in this job?

- What do you see as the most important opportunities for improvement in the area I hope to join?

- What are the attributes of the job performance that you'd like to see improved?

- What attracted you to working for this organization?

- What have you liked most about working here? What improvements would you like to see?

- Are there any weaknesses in the department that you are particularly looking to improve?

- What are the department's goals, and how do they align with the company's mission?

- What goals or objectives need to be achieved in the next six months?

- What areas of the job would you like to see improved when compared to the job done by the person who was most recently performing these duties?

- From all I can see, I'd really like to work here, and I believe I can add considerable value to the company. What's the next step in the selection process?

- What is currently the most pressing business issue or problem for the company or department?

- Would you describe for me the actions of a person who previously achieved success in this position?

- Would you describe for me the action of a person who previously performed poorly in this position?

- What are the most important traits you look for in a subordinate?

- Could you describe to me your typical management style and the type of employee who works well with you?

- How would you describe the experience of working here?

- If I were to be employed here, what one piece of wisdom would you want me to incorporate into my work life?

- What have I yet to learn about this company and opportunity that I still need to know?

- Can you please tell me about the people who will look to me for supervision?

- What happened to the person who previously held this job?

- Customers are expecting companies to protect their data. Does the company have a privacy policy for its Web initiatives, and how does the company balance the momentum for ever-increasing personalization with rising concerns for privacy?

- What are the success factors that will tell you if the decision to bring me on board was the right one?

Other probing questions, especially for high-level assignments

If your prospective assignment is one that inevitably entails additional scrutiny from the first day, some questions will communicate your understanding of your role, the position's importance, and your willingness to protect your position if there are rough patches ahead.

- What are you hoping to accomplish, and what would my role be in those plans?

- What initial projects would I be tackling?

- What sorts of resources would I be able to access to tackle those projects?

- How does the company decide how to allocate those resources?

Mapping Skills to Needs

Consider taking the approach of a consultant. Imagine the company has hired you to give it advice on challenges in the position you seek. Zero in on those challenges. Ask key questions and listen carefully to the answers. If necessary, probe the answers more deeply to unearth potential low-lying problems. Understand the terrain you are asking about. If an answer doesn't clarify your question, ask again in different words until it does. The "stupid question" is often the most important one. It fills an often-critical gap in your comprehension. Additionally, people may pretend you know information when they hope you won't ask about it. Ultimately, make sure you don't leave any elephants in the room—or, if you do, know exactly why you've left them there.

Questions that are defensive

You may have heard or read things about the company that left you with a touch of skepticism, but you still want to apply. There is no guarantee, but some questions can help to protect you as a prospective employee. On-the-job reality may not reflect an interviewer's answers, but at least you will have done your due diligence in advance.

- I understand the company has experienced layoffs within the last two years. Can you review the reasons why they were necessary?

- Are there formal metrics in place for measuring and rewarding employees' performance over time?

- If I was a spectacular success in this position after six months, what would I have accomplished?

- How much freedom would I have in determining my objectives and deadlines?

- How long has this position existed in the organization? Has its scope changed recently?

- Do you foresee this job involving significant amounts of overtime or work on weekends?

- Are my tasks limited to my job description, or will I be performing duties outside the described job scope?

Questions designed to get feedback

With any interviewer, some general questions can help you to judge whether the company is the best fit for you and your career.

Your interviewer may not be willing to give much feedback, but his answers to some open-ended questions can give you a chance to correct his misconceptions or strengthen your response to an earlier question.

- Do you have any concerns about my ability to do the job and fit in?

- How do I compare with the other candidates you have interviewed?

- Is there anything else you need from me to have a complete picture of my qualifications?

Questions to avoid

Sadly, a job interview is not a situation in which there are no stupid questions, only stupid answers. In an interview, there are plenty of stupid questions—questions bad enough to raise an interviewer's hackles, along with her eyebrows.

Here are some suggestions if the goal is an interview that self-destructs. It's not hard to imagine questions that are even less appropriate, but the bottom line is this: any question that asks how little you can contribute at work while still getting by belongs on the list.

- How early can I head home if I've finished my work?

- How sick do I have to be to take the day off?

- Is there a limit on the length of my lunch break?

- Can I come in late without being penalized?

- What sort of drug testing do you do, and when do you do it?

- Will I have to wait for a promotion?

- Are employees allowed to date each other?

- Does the company monitor employees' Internet use, and, if so, how?

Rules of Thumb

Some general principles apply to asking questions of an interviewer, and they are worth bearing in mind as part of your preparation. These principles are:

- Unless you are talking to a recruiter, let the interviewer introduce the topic of compensation. If that topic is not covered, there will be ample time to talk about salary and benefits later in the process—provided, of course, that the interview was enough of a success that "later in the process" comes to pass.

- Keep questions open-ended. Questions that allow for "yes" or "no" answers are conversational dead ends. Instead of asking "Is on-the-job training available?" ask "What kind of training is available?" or "What has proven to be the most useful training for people who have held this position?"

- Avoid questions that are already answered very clearly on the company's website or in its literature.

- On the other hand, ask questions that refer to information that the company has publicized. "I learned from your website that the company plans to expand into a new area. How do you expect that to impact this department and this job? How will people in my position be able to participate in that opportunity?"

- Remember that an interview is about making a sale. You are selling yourself in your resume, your cover letter, and all your interactions with prospective employers. The interview is your chance to close the deal.

- That last point deserves further elaboration and brings up an option that may not suit everyone, since it entails some risk. Consider the sales process. One of the great truisms of selling is that at some point you must actually, explicitly ask for the sale. That same principle leads politicians to close their speeches by explicitly asking for your vote. One way to ask for the sale is to explore the buyer's objections, and you can take that approach in an interview. "Have I said anything here that has hurt my chances?" "What reasons would you have for not offering me the job?" "Are my qualifications enough for the job, or are there things I need to improve?"

These are not questions for the faint of heart, but, like so many questions, they say a lot about the candidate. You welcome feedback, and, it follows, you are interested in improving yourself. At best, your interviewer will appreciate that those qualities are desirable in any employee; at worst, you have learned something you can use next time.

In real estate, as the saying goes, the three most important things are location, location, location. For an interview, the golden rule is similar: the three most important things are preparation, preparation, preparation.

Learn about the company. Visit its website and competitors' sites. Read about the managers. Check the latest news. Prepare your interview answers, but give equal weight to your interview questions. Pick out your interview outfit, and leave plenty of time to get there. Relax, take a deep breath, and smile. Once you're there, remember that, for better or worse, your questions, not your answers, stand to make the strongest impression on that stranger across the table.

CHAPTER 13

A Guide to Salary Negotiation

*The only reason for time is so that
everything doesn't happen at once.*

—Albert Einstein

It may be true that money makes the world go around, but that does not mean we like to talk about it. In 2012, when T. Rowe Price completed its annual survey of almost 2,000 parents and children, it found that some parents feel as awkward talking to their kids about money as they do talking to them about sex or drugs.

Perhaps the survey should be taken with a grain of salt, given that 39 percent of responding parents thought their kids would grow up to be millionaires, but there is no denying its basic truth: money can be an awkward subject in many situations.

Awkward or not, sometimes it is an inevitable subject. Sooner or later, money will be on the table. One context in which the subject of money will always arise is the job interview.

When you know that a topic will be on the interview agenda, the only rational approach to the matter is to prepare. That advice applies to almost every question under the sun, but it is particularly important here, because salary can be one of the trickier interview subjects. Some of the rules that applied to the discussion in the past, when the job market was very healthy, have outlived their usefulness in today's difficult environment. At the moment, the job market is terribly unbalanced. Employers know that any opening will attract a tidal wave of resumes. There is no need to dig deep into applicants' qualifications to find acceptable candidates.

When employers hold all the cards, an applicant may be forced to discuss money much sooner than he might wish. Today, too much resistance to discussing salary can be fatal. To make matters worse, the salary question can kill your chances before your resume even crosses the desk of someone with the power to hire you. You still have options, though, and you can still increase your chances with the right approach.

Your Worth

You may have a very clear idea of what you're worth, or you may have no idea at all—but your own opinions on the matter are, to put it bluntly, irrelevant.

What matters is your prospective employer's perspective, and that is where your preparation should begin. Your employer knows exactly what people at the company are making for similar work, and she probably has a very good idea of what competitors are paying as well.

Your job is to arm yourself with as much of that knowledge as you can. You need to know what companies are typically paying people in your position, and you need to calculate the appropriate salary in light of as many variables as possible.

The two most important data points are education and experience, but bear in mind some other considerations. In many fields, geography can make a difference: the pay scale, along with the cost of living, is higher in a big city than in a small town. The size of the company can also play a part. In other words, be sure you are comparing apples to apples when comparing salaries: an assistant treasurer at a large New York City bank will be making more than his counterpart in Wichita.

Research

There are several possible avenues of research, not all of them of equal value but all worth exploring:

- The single best resource is someone on the inside. If you have a friend in the organization, ask about salary ranges for people in your position. If you have contacts in the industry, ask for their advice.

- If there is no one you can approach directly, reach out to contacts on LinkedIn and Facebook.

- Consult sites such as PayScale, Glassdoor, Vault, and Salary.com, all of which provide a great deal of salary information that can be narrowed by experience, education, location, and company size.

In all of your research, try to consult as many sources as possible. Otherwise, you can end up basing your discussions on the very high or very low end of the scale.

Remember that employers generally base their salary offers on what they themselves are used to paying and on what they think, rightly or wrongly, their competitors are paying. There are sometimes complications, however, such as budget constraints and union pay scales. While some of these factors will remain mysteries, your goal should be to find a range of salaries. Later, you can decide whether to aggressively go for the top of the range or to position yourself lower on the scale.

Reluctant to Ask?

Some job seekers have a misguided tendency to avoid the subject of money, perhaps because they have invested so much energy in portraying themselves as enthusiastic applicants so in love with the work that they would do it for free. That tendency may also mirror one of the standard responses to an interviewer's question about salary. Since the conventional wisdom is to avoid making the first move, the interviewee tries desperately to avoid the question: "I'm focused on the right job in the right place and not so much on the money."

That sort of answer may or may not be a good strategic choice in the interview, but it should not be part of your preparation and research.

In the end, people want and expect to be compensated for their labors, and everyone you approach will understand that salary is a completely natural concern.

The Power Dynamic

Knowledge is power in any negotiation, so knowledge of your salary range is essential, but it's hardly your only source of power. You have to find a way to get whatever leverage you can.

Job seekers may look back wistfully at the days when openings were plentiful and applicants were in demand. New graduates were told to delay salary negotiations until the employer who was their second choice had made an offer, and enter those negotiations armed with that reassuring offer. Now, applicants are not the ones who can pick and choose. Instead, employers have the luxury of seeking the best possible candidate from a flood of candidates. It is no longer enough to be someone who can do a competent job.

The burden is on applicants to prove their worth, and that proof starts with a clear understanding of the job, the company, and the industry, along with a detailed assessment of your qualifications. Learn as much as you can about the job and the company. If you are taking over for someone else, what are that person's qualifications? What are her responsibilities? Do you bring more to the table? If this is a new position, what are the company's expectations? Can you exceed those expectations?

Above all, can you demonstrate the value that you will bring to the company? When it comes to salary, you must demonstrate that you are worth what you expect to be paid.

If you can quantify that worth, for example by demonstrating what you'll add to the organization's bottom line, so much the better. Even if you can't draw a direct line between your job and increased revenue or lower costs, focus on the skills that make a difference for the organization. Keep that principle in mind when thinking about your approach to the salary question.

Discussing Salary Before the Interview

Employers do not always wait until the day of the interview to raise the salary issue. They often ask one of two questions, and sometimes they will ask both:

- What was your previous salary?

- What is your desired salary?

Should you disclose what you made in the past? Should you provide a desired salary?

It is in your best interest to offer no information at all, and there are two reasons to keep quiet.

First, unless the job has been posted with an anticipated salary range, you have no way of knowing what the employer plans to pay. If you set your sights too high, you can end up among the discards, because the employer can't afford you. If you set them too low, the employer may conclude that you're not qualified for the job. Worst of all, these are the kinds of decisions that can be made automatically, before anyone has really looked at your resume.

Second, in any negotiation, it is better to leave the onus on the other side to come up with an opening number. By putting a number on the table, you may be selling yourself short by setting the terms of the salary negotiation in too low a range.

Sometimes, the salary question is part of an application form. When asked about your previous salary, write "competitive" rather than filling in a number. When asked about desired salary, use "negotiable."

There are some applications that demand salary information in no uncertain terms: "YOUR APPLICATION WILL BE DISCARDED IF YOU FAIL TO INCLUDE COMPLETE SALARY INFORMATION." Obviously, that leaves the applicant in a difficult position. The best option is to find a way to get your application in front of a hiring manager directly, and that may put your networking skills to the test. If you can't get around the question, and you choose to provide numbers, be honest about the past and be smart about your expectations. This is a time when your research into company and industry-wide salaries can pay dividends.

The salary question may also come up during preliminary screening. In that case, the best option is to defer questions as best you can but be prepared to surrender. Refusing to answer has become increasingly dangerous.

Here's why: With a glut of qualified applicants, the first thing on an employer's mind is narrowing the field, quickly and inexpensively. With so many applicants, there is little or nothing to be gained by conducting in-depth screening of candidates early in the process.

As a result, employers have delegated that task to relatively low-level screeners, people who typically have no power to make decisions. Those screeners are, however, provided with simple criteria for passing applicants along to the next round. Their job is to ask simple questions, not to make judgment calls, and nothing is simpler than salary. They don't have to think. You are either within the range or ready for relegation to the discard pile.

When screeners are provided with the relevant numbers and instructed to toss out everyone who expects to earn more than the cutoff, there are no gray areas. Nothing could be simpler than to have the screener ask for a number, insist on getting it, and discard everyone who refuses to answer or whose answer is outside the limits.

For the applicant, the problem is that you don't really know where those limits have been set. All is not lost, though. You should at least be able to make an educated guess, based on the research you have done, even if you don't know the range for sure.

You can also turn the question around. "My salary range will depend on some specifics about the job. Do you have a range that you've budgeted for the position?"

My clients get an answer to that question in approximately half of all screening interviews, and it's a huge help. Once you do, you can say that you are comfortable with the salary range. You can say that because the range itself doesn't really matter. By going along with the screener, you haven't committed yourself to anything. The subject can be addressed in detail down the road, and sometimes the next interview in which you discuss salary is months ahead. At the moment, your goal is simply to move on to the next round.

If you can't elicit more information from the screener, set your range low. Use the information you have obtained, pick a broad range, and consider setting the top of your range some 15 percent below your true ambitions. Again, you have not locked yourself into that range or into any number. There will be plenty of time to talk about the actual salary that you're willing to accept. For now, your aim has not changed in the slightest: avoid being disqualified.

If it's later in the process, or if you are willing to take a risk during preliminary screening, you can try to avoid the subject for as long as possible, and here are two ways to defer the conversation:

- I'm very interested in the position. Perhaps we can discuss compensation when we meet. I'm sure that it won't be an issue.

- Before speaking with you, I'd done a lot of research into the industry and your company, and there seems to be a wide range of pay, with a number of things that determine salary. First, I'd like to get a more complete idea of the responsibilities of the job. Then I'll know what range makes sense.

Sooner or later, people will dig in their heels. An interviewer, whether a preliminary screener or not, may refuse to pass you on to the next level unless you tackle the issue. Deferring discussion of your desired future compensation may be a lost cause at that point, but you can still try to defer discussion of the past with one of two possible responses.

Neither response will apply to everyone, but they can be reasonable options if they do apply:

- I didn't provide my previous pay because I've spent the last two years as an independent contractor. My freelance rates would turn into an annual salary of at least $250,000, and I didn't see that as the equivalent of a salary history or as a figure that would necessarily be relevant here.

- My present employer has all employees sign a non-disclosure agreement, and that agreement specifically covers questions of compensation. I can't go into salary specifics without violating that NDA, but I'm sure that we'll be able to agree on a number when the time comes.

All the delays and excuses in the world may not save you in the end. Employers have the right to ask about your salary history, and at some point you may have to accede to their wishes—gracefully, of course. The first principle of salary disclosure is to be honest. An inflated salary history is not your friend, especially when employers can ask for documentation.

There are, however, some situations that call for special treatment:

- A salary history well above current market rates can give employers pause. They assume you won't be happy at a lower salary. Let them know that you understand their concern and that you know times have changed.

The tough economy has caused salaries to decrease across the board, and that applies to your field as much as any.

- An under-market salary is sometimes less of a problem. After all, it is a perfectly acceptable reason to be looking for a better job.

- If a history of a relatively low salary is a problem, present your history as a total compensation package. Include base pay, bonuses, variable pay, and indirect pay. Assign values to benefits, which typically add around 50 percent to your nominal salary. There may be other reasons for your low salary. You may have been working at a smaller company or in a place where pay scales are lower.

When Push Comes to Shove

In every job in which compensation is not determined by a force beyond everyone's control, numbers will be on the table sooner or later. Before considering specific strategies, remember to keep the principle of value in mind. Enter the negotiation with a clear sense of the qualities that are important to the job and the ways in which you represent those qualities, particularly the ways in which you are different from—and, ideally, superior to—other candidates.

You also need a clear sense of what you want. What is the least you are willing to accept? What is the most you would hope for? Those numbers will play an important part in your negotiation.

Stonewalling

You may have reached the final interview, but there is still no reason to start throwing numbers around. Continue to focus on the other aspects of the job that are important to you. This approach can make for some awkward interview moments, but those moments will not derail the process if you are honest, diplomatic, and positive.

Remember, too, that silence can be golden. If you have told the interviewer that you are more concerned with your role and the job's potential than with the rate of pay, let that answer suffice. Be willing to wait for the interviewer to respond. Do not feel compelled to fill every pause. Silence is one of the negotiator's most effective tools.

In the end, you can try one more tactic that can put a bit of the burden on the interviewer, and that tactic revolves around the question of where you stand within the hierarchy of applicants.

Ask about other candidates who might be under serious consideration. If there are several people in the running, ask how you compare. Your interviewer may well be willing to discuss your relative strengths and weaknesses. In the interview itself, your question can put you on a more collegial level with the interviewer, and it can help the interview seem more like a conversation than a question-and-answer session. Don't feel pressed to respond immediately, but do consider writing to the interviewer after the fact and addressing the weaknesses he raises.

If you are the top candidate, the inevitable can no longer be postponed, but there are still two possible variations on the process. In either case, someone will have to state a figure.

The Interviewer Blinks

If you have managed to coax the first offer from the interviewer, compare it to your minimum and maximum expectations. Even if it comes in at the top of your anticipated range, don't leap to accept it. This is, after all, a negotiation, and almost all employers expect candidates to counter their proposals.

This is a situation that does not call for an immediate response. By all means, make it clear that you are happy to have received the offer, but say that you will respond in a day. This is not the time to offer excuses for the delay, especially if you are tempted to attribute it to the need to discuss things with your spouse. You want to convey the impression of someone who is thoughtful and decisive, someone who considers big decisions seriously. You do not want to seem that you are not in control of your career.

When you do respond, ask about the employer's rationale. How did they arrive at the number? What factors did they consider?

With that information and with your own research in mind, explain your rationale for a higher salary. Perhaps the industry in general pays a few thousand dollars more for the position. Perhaps you have been offered a salary that is typical for people with your education or experience, but you bring something extra to the table that the employer has not factored into the offer. Make it specific, and tie it to the benefits that the employer will realize. The idea is that the additional cost of hiring you will pay for itself in measurable ways. That's why you're worth more.

If you are offered a range instead of a single number, take a similar approach but add a small variation. Ask for a day to think it over, but do one thing differently: When you hear the range that the employer proposes, ignore everything except the top of the range. For example, the employer says, "We've budgeted eighty to ninety thousand dollars for the position." Only respond to the higher number: "Hmm, ninety thousand dollars." Express your gratitude and ask for time to consider. It's the higher number that should be the focus of attention.

The Interviewee's Range

All is not lost in a negotiation if you are forced to make the first move. It gives you the opportunity to "anchor" the negotiation, and a few experts actually prefer it as a strategy.

Speaking First

Most experts recommend that applicants do everything possible to avoid making the first offer, but there are some who disagree. Those in the "speak first" camp tend to rely on the anchoring effect to support their argument, and it's fair to say that the effect is real and that it offers some consolation for candidates forced to make the first move.

However, the effect does not influence all situations equally, and salary negotiations, especially in a difficult market, are not the best place for the effect to work its magic. Consider the way the effect works in home sales, one of the frequently used examples of its power. There, the idea is that a high listing price moves every buyer's sights higher. Let's say, though, that there are few buyers out there and plenty of houses for sale in the neighborhood. Instead of bringing higher offers, a high listing price is likely to encourage buyers to simply move on to the next house.

That is the situation in today's job market. Employers have large pools of applicants from which to choose. A candidate who tries to anchor the negotiation at a high price may find that the employer simply moves on to the next applicant. When the job market improves and applicants are scarce, make the first move. Until then, resist making the first offer for as long as you can.

The anchoring effect relies on the tendency of people to be influenced by any number that enters a negotiation. Adam Galinsky, a professor at the Kellogg School of Management, explains that anchor numbers "pull judgments toward themselves." That phenomenon is the reason for focusing only on the higher number when an employer offers a range of salaries. When you are the one making the first offer, you want to anchor the discussion at the high end of your range, perhaps 10 to 15 percent above your most optimistic and pessimistic outcomes.

One interesting effect of a high anchor is that, according to Galinsky, it "selectively directs our attention toward an item's positive attributes." In other words, people unconsciously look for the reasons that justify the high value, while minimizing negatives that might attach to a low value. Although much of the research into anchors has dealt with specific physical products, those effects are precisely the ones that an applicant may want to put into play.

In addition to its anchoring effect, setting your offer high gives you the benefit of leeway in the negotiation. It allows you to bargain for other types of compensation, such as benefits and vacation time, that are very real nonmonetary workplace rewards.

Regardless of your exact figures, some principles always apply. Be prepared to justify the offer, using the same information and research that you have already brought to bear on the negotiation, and make your justification as concrete as possible.

You may also want to consider offering a relatively wide range, if only so that you don't disqualify yourself completely.

Assuming that you haven't priced yourself completely out of the market—and there's no reason for that to happen if you've done your homework—there is really only one serious mistake that you can make in salary negotiations.

You make that mistake when you fail to explain yourself. You can, of course, simply throw out a number and hope that someone bites, but that's hardly a strategy. No employer will rise to the bait. They will pay you more if they think you're worth more, but you have to convince them that they've underestimated your value. Show them what they've missed. Show them you can do even more for them than they expected. Show them why they should positively want to pay you more than they had thought.

If you can do that, a higher salary is the product of a sound business decision, and, as a result, it's simply a good deal for everyone. That's how the conversation should be framed.

Tips

- Get it in writing. If all goes well, you will have arrived at a mutually satisfactory conclusion. The parties will shake hands and congratulate each other. It's not quite time, though, to give notice at your old job or start spending the money you are about to make. Job offers, complete with details on compensation, need to be in writing before you can rely on them. Nothing is final until everyone has signed on the dotted line.

- Talk to the right people. If you are trying to arrange some creative alternatives to make up for a salary that is not quite what you wanted, negotiating with hiring managers and HR staff may not be the best route. Whenever your proposal departs from the standard options to any meaningful degree, try to negotiate with people who are outside of HR and who have more authority to bend the rules. Even simple departures from routine can be difficult for procedure-bound HR departments. For example, say you do not need the company's health insurance because you are covered by your spouse's policy, and you would like something in return. A hiring manager may be baffled, but a COO may be able to manage the trade.

- A low offer may be bearable. If the employer is not budging from an offer that is barely in your acceptable range, talk about the future. Focus on what happens after you are hired. What opportunities will you have? How will you be evaluated? Are there formal procedures for advancement? How are salary increases determined?

- This is not a fight. There is only one thing on which negotiation experts always agree: The best outcomes are the ones in which all parties are reasonably satisfied with the outcome. These are the win-win negotiations. The principle is particularly important in a negotiation that will be followed by an extended period of time in which the parties will be working together. It's all too easy to establish a reputation as someone who is bound to be an impossible colleague. As Harvard Business School professor Kathleen McGinn put it, "You don't want to negotiate so hard that people are sick of you before your first day."[1]

Do's and Don'ts

Do:

- research salaries thoroughly beforehand
- use several sources for that research

- if pressed by screeners, be prepared to offer a range, but be conservative

- keep nonmonetary compensation in mind when negotiating

- be prepared to justify your position

- make suggestions

- get it in writing

Don't:

- inflate your salary history

- ignore nonmonetary compensation if your salary history is below market

- make the first offer if you can avoid it

- take the employer's first offer

- make demands

CHAPTER 14

More Linchpins for Success

*The most certain way to succeed is
always to try just one more time.*
—Thomas Edison

Preparation heightens your confidence, fills out interviews like wind in a sail, and gives solid evidence of your work caliber. If you are prepared, you will be more relaxed, because you will know the terrain. You will have anticipated the key inquiries, have your answers ready, and have plenty of questions of your own. You will know exactly how you can benefit the company, and you can subtly guide the interview to these points. You will know that surprises are much less likely and that you can deal with them when they come. You won't be walking into a maze. There are special circumstances, though, where you may need to do some things a little differently.

You Are a Veteran

If you're a veteran who has recently left the service and you're on the hunt for a civilian job, you can certainly rely on the general advice that applies to all interviews. There's nothing there that doesn't apply to you, but there are a few special points that you should bear in mind. In the end, everything revolves around adjusting to the ways of the civilian world:

- As a preliminary matter, don't limit yourself. It's natural for veterans to look for work in the defense industry. Broaden your horizons to include the whole range of commercial and governmental possibilities.

- Jargon plays a major part in military life, as it does in many highly systematized and specialized organizations. Use it as little as possible, especially if you're not completely sure that civilian usage is identical.

- Along with its fondness for jargon, the military loves acronyms with a passion. Civilians, however, especially those with no military background, will be baffled by anything beyond acronyms that have entered ordinary language. They will understand SNAFU, but anything more will leave them in the dark. Never assume that an acronym will be understood. Use the full phrase and, if it's still not clear, put it in terms that are easily understood.

- Emphasize accomplishments, not titles. Interviewers will not know the difference between a chief warrant officer 2 and a staff sergeant. If you left the army as a brigadier general, by all means use the title. Everyone else should focus on the responsibilities of the rank and the work it entailed.

- Translate. The bottom line is that your job in the interview is to translate your military experience into civilian terms, in the same way that someone would translate from one language to another. Don't hesitate to ask an interviewer if your translation was clear enough.

- Brag. In the service, modesty is encouraged, sometimes explicitly and sometimes because that's just the way things are done. What might seem like excessive self-promotion in the service is the very thing that's needed in the job interview. After all, you're selling yourself.

- Use "sir" and "ma'am" in moderation. Obviously, it becomes a habit in the service. If it doesn't, you'll have problems. It's not part of the natural speech pattern in the civilian world, though, and it can put some interviewers off.

One thing military service provides is the chance to take supervisory responsibility faster than most people do in civilian occupations. That can be a real selling point, so don't forget to use it.

You Have an Accent
If you are not a native speaker of English, you may have a noticeable accent even if you are perfectly fluent in the language. That accent should not be a problem unless you are completely oblivious to it. If you are aware of it, especially

if you are aware that people sometimes have difficulty understanding you, the best approach is to acknowledge that fact to the interviewer on your own, early in the process, before it interferes with communication.

"I know that I have an accent. Sometimes when people first meet me they may have a bit of a hard time understanding everything I say. I am fluent, but accents don't disappear so easily. I'm happy to repeat myself at any time, so please feel free to let me know if anything is unclear. On the job, people get used to my accent pretty quickly, and it's never been a problem for me or my colleagues."

Acknowledging the issue can put the interviewer at ease, and it addresses an issue before it becomes the issue.

In any case, it can be hard for the speaker to judge whether an accent is truly problematic. The best approach is to watch for difficulties when you practice interviewing. Practice with a real person, and encourage that person to point out any bumps in the road.

This advice also applies to native English speakers with pronounced regional accents. If you've spent your life in Glasgow and are interviewing in Mississippi, evaluate your accent in advance, preferably with an American Southerner. Don't forget that Americans sometimes complain about the lack of subtitles in British film and television. Dialects and accents, even when two native English speakers meet, can interfere with effective communication.

You Have a Disability

It may be self-evident that disabled people have to overcome obstacles on a daily basis, but the job interview presents some extra challenges. You need to be prepared, and that requires some strategic consideration of the following:

- The Americans with Disabilities Act (ADA) outlaws discrimination against people with disabilities. That's a good thing, but it has at least one potentially negative consequence in the interview: Interviewers may be uncomfortable. They may be wary of asking questions that violate the ADA. Conversation becomes awkward. As if you didn't have enough on your mind, it becomes your job to put the interviewer at ease. The best approach is to be friendly and relaxed. Keep it professional, but remember that a little humor can go a long way toward breaking the ice.

- If you have a visible disability, address it head-on. Put yourself in the interviewer's place. What might she be worried about? What kinds of problems does she anticipate? Then, raise the issue yourself. "You may be worried about my ability to do one of the tasks that's part of the job, and I understand your concern, but here's something you may not know about the things I can do. Here's why that will not be an issue for me."

- Interviewers may not realize that the ADA gives them some latitude in determining your ability to perform job-related tasks. Don't assume that they have no concerns simply because they haven't raised them. Sometimes, you have to take the lead.

- If your disability is invisible, you do not have to disclose it, nor do you have to disclose any need for accommodation. It is perfectly legitimate to hold off disclosing anything until you have a job offer in hand. If you choose, and if it fits your situation, it is equally legitimate for you to never make those disclosures.

- Regardless of the strategy you choose, keep one thing in mind: You are a person with talents and skills who, by the way, has a disability. You are not a person with a disability who happens to have some talents and skills. The distinction is critical.

You Have Jumped from Job to Job

Your resume is the place to start. If you've moved from job to job, and you're not sure how to present yourself, a good resume writer can help. You may need a functional resume or a resume that makes dates a little less prominent—and does it gracefully. The question of frequent job changes is likely to come up in an interview, though, and it needs to be addressed there. The first thing to remember is that you made it to this stage despite your nomadic ways. You haven't been immediately disqualified, so they must be seeing something they like. Use the following as your guide:

- Given that you've come this far, don't make this a bigger issue than it already is. Changing jobs is something that happens. Focus on the positive things that are central to marketing yourself.

- Why have you changed jobs so often? Companies go out of business. They downsize. If that's what happened, make it clear that the changes were not of your doing.

- If your reasons were more personal, look for the positives. You received a better offer. You changed direction. When this is the case, try not to give the impression that you'll have one foot out the door as soon as you're hired.

- If your reasons were negative, do your best to avoid bad-mouthing former employers or former colleagues. Otherwise, an interviewer will be tempted to look at you as a potential negative influence in the workplace. Even if you are the world's most difficult person and you've never gotten along with a single fellow employee, that's not the image you want to project.

- Remember that frequent job changes are fairly common in today's economy. Employers know this. It is not the terrible black mark that it once was.

You Have Been Fired

You've been fired, and perhaps it's happened more than once. You didn't lose your job because the business collapsed or laid people off. You weren't caught in the undertow of something bigger than you. This is hardly ideal, but perhaps it's not the end of the world, because, strangely enough, this employer wants to talk to you. You have something that caught the company's eye, but you know you will have to deal with your checkered past in the interview. A prospective employer will certainly want to know what happened.

Your goal is to limit the damage. The following tips can help you achieve that goal:

- Don't be tempted into giving long, elaborate answers. Keep it simple and direct. Try to portray the firing as an isolated incident, not a global reflection of your skills. For example, talk about a problem your boss had getting along with you. Make it clear that you didn't have that problem with other people and that your work itself did not suffer.

- At the same time, don't spend time criticizing your old employer or your old colleagues. If you do, you're simply inviting the interviewer to see you as a negative influence in your workplace.

- Instead of saying you were "fired," make things a bit less personal: "My position was terminated."

- Talk about the firing as a learning experience. Acknowledge that there was a problem and that you may not have handled it in the best way at the time. Make it clear, though, that the experience taught you important lessons. Try to be as specific as possible, and emphasize the ways in which your experience will help you to make an even greater contribution to this organization.

You've Spent a Long Time at One Job

You've been in the same job forever. Your long tenure has a positive side: You're stable and able to commit yourself for the long term. An interviewer may see another side to your career, though, and wonder about your flexibility. Will you be able to adjust to a new environment? Will you be one of those people who dwell on how things were done at your old job? Can you deal with a new way of doing things, or was the way you did things for so many years the only way?

In the interview, emphasize your flexibility and your willingness to change. To add credibility, describe specific instances in your past that support those qualities. You've met challenges in the past, you're open to new ideas, and you're excited about new opportunities.

The most convincing approach involves connecting those new opportunities to this new employer, and that means doing your homework before the interview. Research the new company and identify the areas that represent real changes from your previous job. Again, the best responses are the most specific.

You're Worried About the A-G-E Factor

Age discrimination is a reality. Since it is illegal, no one will admit to it, but you have to consider its impact on your job search. Thinking about it is not enough. You have to take steps to minimize its influence on your prospects:

- Is there an assumption that you're more expensive because you're older? Nip it in the bud. Make it clear that your salary expectations are within normal limits and that you're flexible.

- Is the employer's real worry that you are overqualified? If so, deal with that issue head-on.

- Are you looking your age or, in the worst case, more than your age? You don't need to schedule immediate plastic surgery, but if that suit you're wearing is your favorite from 25 years ago, it's time for a moderate wardrobe investment.

- Are you yourself uncomfortable with the situation? You may have a hard time accepting authority figures who are young enough to be your children, and that attitude may be communicating itself to a younger interviewer.

Pick your battles wisely. Some industries and some employers are more youth oriented than others, and there comes a time when you may need to cut your losses and move on to another option—if, that is, you're looking for a job and not an opportunity to litigate a discrimination claim.

It is also worth remembering that not all age discrimination is illegal. Can employers ask how old you are? Yes, but they can't use that information as their reason for not hiring you. Are there exceptions to that rule? Yes, because age can be a perfectly legal reason if it has a legitimate connection to the job. These are some fairly subtle distinctions, the kind of distinctions that make proving discrimination difficult, and the best option for most applicants is to move on.

You're Concerned You Don't Look the Part

We humans are terribly shallow creatures. We judge books by their covers. We make snap judgments. We base decisions on first impressions. Hiring managers are famously likely to decide if a candidate is a probable hire within the first couple of minutes of meeting that person.

We can bemoan that situation, or we can see it as just one more fact to deal with in the job hunt. To deal with it effectively, keep some simple rules in mind:

For everyone

- Unless you are given explicit instructions to the contrary, stick to formal, businesslike attire even if you are expecting to interview on the office's weekly bikini day.

- Your look can be contemporary, but avoid the avant-garde unless you're visiting an avant-garde fashion house.

- Wear a dark suit in a solid color.

- Although they may have lost their transgressive aura and become increasingly common, keep tattoos hidden.

- Keep it clean. Shower the morning of the interview and use deodorant.

- Give yourself a last look in the mirror before you arrive.

For men

- Shave the day of the interview.

- Consider a haircut a few days before the event.

- Avoid sandals and sneakers.

- Wear leather shoes and give them a shine.

- Wear a conservative tie.

- Make sure your nails are neatly trimmed.

For women

- Go easy on the makeup and perfume.

- Avoid excessive or flashy jewelry.

- Avoid clothing that is too revealing.

- Wear your hair in a neat, simple, and professional style.

- Make sure your nails are manicured and polish is simple.

An interview doesn't give you much chance to express your individuality through the way you dress. Show off your unique style once you have the job, but think of dressing for the interview as a sort of camouflage. You won't get the job because of the way you dress, but you can lose the job for that very reason. When all is said and done, you want your interviewer to remember you for something other than your wardrobe.

Keeping Calm and Carrying On

No job seeker needs to be reminded that this is a tough job market, and many people can expect a hard lesson in handling rejection to be part of the job search. In a healthy market, that lesson is usually learned by people who have made a mess of the process. Their resumes are incoherent, their cover letters are filled with typos, and their references have only the most painful memories to share.

Today, even if you have done everything right, and even if you have had the best professional help with your presentation, there are no guarantees. By any reasonable standard, you are a compelling candidate. Your resume clearly sets out your skills and accomplishments and your increasing responsibility, and everything makes it abundantly obvious that you are a perfect fit for the job.

Still, it turns out that an interview is not in the cards. You have done a fine job selling yourself, but the company is not buying, and the fact that you are selling yourself is what can make this moment so painful. Put your car on the market, and it's not hard to cope with the notion that not everyone wants to buy it. Put yourself on the market, and you can adopt the tagline from the fourth installment of the *Jaws* movie franchise as your motto: "This time it's personal."

Before you let discouragement take over, pause for a moment to reflect on the possibility that the lack of an interview may not be so personal after all. Employers have all sorts of reasons for ignoring someone who would impress an objective observer.

The Inside Pitch

One of the toughest competitors for someone applying from outside a company is someone inside the company. That person is a known quantity, an outsider is a riskier bet, and employers, to no one's surprise, are a risk-averse lot. In government hiring, there is often a legal requirement that jobs be advertised publicly, even when a decision has already been made to hire from within.

The Son Also Rises

Nepotism has a bad name, but employers, especially in the private sector, are free to hire from a pool of relatives and friends, however incompetent. The best resume and the best networking cannot compete with the candidate who joins the boss at Thanksgiving dinner every year or the one brought in by a friendly department head.

Job? What Job?

Legal or not, it's not unheard of for a job to be posted when there is, in fact, no such opening. This is more of a problem with agencies than with employers themselves. Agencies occasionally decide that it is worth posting a job in order to increase their pool of registered job seekers. Companies have been known to do it to test the waters.

The Very Best and Very Brightest

A struggling economy and a sputtering job market have a profound effect on the applicant pool. Accomplishments that would have awed employers five years ago are now judged against extraordinary competition. You were last year's champion at the local club, but this year Tiger Woods decided to join. It's not so bad to be this year's runner-up on the links, but coming close in the job search is cold comfort at best.

Along with everything else, remember that employers make mistakes. In this market, some of the best fail to make the cut, and, in a very real sense, it's not personal after all. Sit down with a professional and take another look at your resume. Tweak it if necessary, but keep moving forward.

Fred Astaire was looking for a job long ago. A screen test was part of the hiring process, and the expert opinion was succinct: "Can't act. Slightly bald. Also dances." Fred may have been hurt, but he kept dancing, and his persistence paid off. Sooner or later, we all have to find ways to follow in his nimble footsteps.

CHAPTER 15

The Ideal Interview

The ideal life is in our blood and never will be still.
—Phillips Brooks

S o, now you know how to avoid interview mistakes and how to prepare for the only interview question you must be able to answer. We've looked at how you should dress, how you should talk about salary, the best way to answer weird questions, and the kind of questions you should ask.

To recap this wealth of information and advice, let's imagine what would happen if all of those elements came together in one interview. What does the ideal interview look like? What is the perfect interview that applicants dream of? Does such a thing exist, or is it only theoretical?

It's easy to get caught up in thoughts of all that can go wrong in the interview, and such a state of mind can make the experience much more nerve-racking than it has to be. Whether or not the ideal interview is only theoretical, people *do* have success. They get hired. Mere mortals ace their interviews. What happens when everything clicks?

Before the Interview

An interview does not happen in a vacuum. It has a context. You may have heard this a thousand times, but it bears repeating, because everything flows from this simple axiom: In an interview, your job is to sell yourself. Everything that happens in the ideal interview is a matter of doing that job well. Every applicant should remind himself of that context at every opportunity.

This doesn't mean the interviewee has to do a hard sell. Instead, a successful interview is an accumulation of small steps on the interviewee's part, all of which contribute to making a persuasive case.

Lawyers spend their time attempting the same feat. They try to make persuasive cases, and they all agree that the most important determinant of success or failure is not silver-tongued oratory or the ability to tie a witness in knots. The most important task is preparation. As Abe Lincoln, a well-known member of the Illinois bar, put it, "If I had eight hours to chop down a tree, I'd spend six sharpening my axe."

So the perfect interviewee prepares thoroughly, but what does that mean in practical terms?

Without lapsing into undue cynicism, it means projecting a certain image, and the nature of that image governs the nature of your preparation. How do you want to be perceived?

You want to be seen as:

- smart

- knowledgeable

- enthusiastic

- engaged

- hardworking

- responsible

- reliable

- competent

- personable

The list of adjectives that describe an ideal candidate could extend for pages, and there are some specific qualities that would be ideal for specific jobs, but the general idea is that you, the perfect candidate, will make a perfect employee.

To establish that aura of perfection, there are three distinct components of preparation: research, practice, and appearance:

- Perfect research means you learn about the industry and the company. It means you understand the company's history, its place in the industry now, and the challenges it faces. It means you know how the company has met those challenges, even if some of its efforts have been unsuccessful. It means you know your anticipated role in the company and its culture.

- Perfect practice means you take the time to rehearse the interview. It means that you devise a thorough list of interview questions and use your research to prepare some questions of your own. It means that you actually sit down with someone and play the part, asking and answering questions in an environment that simulates the interview as closely as possible. Finally, you record a practice session, which helps you to eliminate many small flaws that you would never notice without the help of a camera. You encourage your interviewer to provide some feedback on your physical appearance, posture, and body language. We are often unable to see ourselves as others see us; and painful though it may be, it pays to identify problems before the big day.

- Perfect appearance means you dress and are groomed for the occasion, because you understand the importance of first impressions. Your outfit, neither frumpy nor overly stylish, fits right in with the way the company's employees dress. Strangely enough, perfection means looking like someone who doesn't need a job.

First Impressions

The big day finally arrives. Since you know you could not have prepared any better, you are quietly confident.

You bear in mind the mantra of the interview: all things in moderation. Those words apply to everything, from the timing of your arrival to the strength of your handshake. You've been moderate in the fragrance, makeup, or after-shave you're wearing.

Your appearance and body language are remarkably important. Some hiring managers acknowledge that it takes only 30 seconds to determine if an interviewee is an acceptable candidate. First impressions matter, and physical behavior is an influence throughout the interview. It may be irrational and unfair, but the wrong look can derail your candidacy even if your questions and answers are exemplary.

You're looking your best. In your briefcase, you have copies of your resume and any other paperwork you might be asked about.

You arrive a few minutes early. You introduce yourself to the receptionist and make a bit of pleasant small talk. You call her by name. You want to make a good impression on everyone you meet, not only because that's your natural inclination but also because you never know who has the ear of decision makers.

When you meet the person who will conduct the interview, you smile, make good eye contact, and shake hands. Your handshake is neither bone crushing nor like a dead fish. Throughout the interview, you remember that eye contact is important. If there is more than one interviewer, you give each person some of your attention.

Everything about your presentation reinforces that you are alert, engaged, focused, and professional.

When you sit down, you are aware of your body language. You don't fidget or distractedly look around the room. You're not slumped in your chair. You don't repeatedly touch your face or hair. You sit up straight, perhaps leaning slightly forward, toward your interviewer.

Not one word of substance has been said, but you have made the impression you set out to make: of an alert and engaged employee. At the very least, nothing you have done has sabotaged your chances before the questions and answers have even begun, and you're not expecting to be hired in spite of first impressions.

Interviewers have different approaches to the start of the interview. Some are much more inclined to make small talk than others. You can use that to your advantage if you follow the interviewer's lead. Keep the conversation going and don't hesitate to ask a question or two. If you're in the interviewer's personal office, you may find clues to his interests in your surroundings. When you leave the interview, you'd like the interviewer to see you as someone who would make a wonderful colleague, someone with whom he'd just had an interesting and rewarding conversation.

The "Real" Interview

You're more than happy to begin the part of the process that people think of as the "real" interview now. Since you have prepared so thoroughly, nothing takes you by surprise.

The first question is an old chestnut: Why do you want to work at XYZ Company?

Listen to the question before leaping to answer. This question may be utterly standard, but interviewees have been known to lose sight of what's actually being asked. In the back of your mind, you should think about your answer as a response to the qualities the company highlighted in its job posting—or, if the posting doesn't provide enough information, to the qualities that are naturally pertinent to the position, the company, and the industry.

"As you know, I've been at ABC Company for the past five years, and I've advanced from junior assistant to department manager. I've accomplished a great deal at ABC, especially in the area of risk evaluation process, and I've found my work interesting and rewarding. At the same time, I've been aware of XYZ and the cutting-edge work you're doing with automated evaluations, a field that's really exciting to me.

"At ABC, I was able to reduce exposure to catastrophic eventualities by almost a third, at the same time increasing retention and premium flow-through. ABC, however, has been focused on the consumer segment, which is certainly an important component of the market, but XYZ has been moving more and more into commercial applications. I think that's where the real potential is, and I'd love to be a part of it and bring my skills to an area that looks like the future of the industry."

It's a long answer—and, for the purposes of this example, laden with fabricated jargon—but this is an important question. The answer has the virtue of specificity. You don't talk in terms of "people skills" or "team players." You talk knowledgeably about the new company, give concrete reasons for its appeal, and, at the same time, avoid saying anything negative about ABC. You show awareness of current issues and demonstrate success in confronting those issues. You give evidence of quantifiable accomplishments.

"Tell me about a problem you faced at ABC," the interviewer says next.

"I had been at ABC for about two years and had recently been promoted to team leader. I learned there was one very large customer who was becoming unhappy with ABC. The word was that she was looking seriously at other companies, but we didn't have a clear idea of what the problem was. I met with the team and then I met with each team member, but everyone seemed to be mystified.

"Finally, after getting the okay from my manager, I went directly to the client, and I decided to meet with her in person. I found that she had problems with one particular team member, someone with excellent technical skills but no gift for customer service. We resolved the situation, and the team member was actually happier to be out of the situation. The customer was happy, too, and we ended up increasing the amount of business we were doing with her over the next year."

"What did you take away from that situation?" the interviewer asks.

"The situation was made more difficult because it was not addressed quickly enough. I learned that situations like this need to be resolved before they degenerate. Nobody wants to deal with difficult clients, and it can be too easy to accept the idea that the cause of the difficulty is a mystery. At that point, you can end up doing nothing and hoping for the best. It reinforced in my mind the necessity of being proactive and looking a little harder at things that might not be going as well as they could."

Questions about weaknesses and difficulties should not be treated as opportunities to elaborate on every problem you might have. You are expected to be human and make mistakes; the ability to learn from those mistakes is what really matters. With this answer, you shoulder some of the responsibility for the situation—instead of bad-mouthing coworkers—and explain what you did to reach a good result. A difficulty thus becomes a strength.

The interview continues in this vein, but the format begins to change. At first, you listen to short questions that come from the interviewer's standard playbook, and you provide relatively long answers. As time goes on, the interviewer departs from the playbook. He picks up on one of your answers and talks about a new program that the company is starting. You offer your thoughts. There is more give-and-take. You begin to feel that the interview has turned from interrogation to conversation.

That is exactly what the ideal interview should be: a conversation. If everyone is sufficiently engaged, you may even start to lose track of the amount of time you've been there.

Take the Long-Term View

No matter how enticing the position, don't center your existence on it. Understand that the company never would have invited you in if you weren't a serious candidate, one who could plainly advance the firm. The interview is a mutual sounding-out process, so take your assessment role seriously. You don't want to wind up in a political shark tank, for instance, or in a harsh corporate culture where tiny mistakes earn criticism and success earns little. The company will be selling itself to you, and you don't have to buy. Fit goes both ways.

Your Turn to Ask Questions

You sense that the interview is winding down, but you know there will be one more question from the interviewer. He doesn't disappoint you.

"Do you have any questions for me?"

How you respond to this invitation is as important as any other part of the interview. In the ideal interview, you will have answered many questions already, but there are always topics that do not get covered. Your questions can underline your interest and engagement in a general way, but they can also do that more specifically. You are not here for just any job. You are here for this job with this company. You consider yourself a serious candidate, and your questions should reinforce that impression.

You know that you can ask questions from three categories: questions about the interviewer; questions about the company and your future there; and questions about your application. If time permits, you'll ask something from each category.

About the interviewer: "What led you to work at XYZ? What keeps you here?"

About the company and your future there: "What are the company's priorities for the position? What results would you expect within my first couple of months?"

About your application: "Was there anything in my resume I can clarify for you? Can I offer any follow-up that would be helpful?"

You find that the interviewer's response to each of these questions brings to mind one or two follow-up questions, but you don't ask them all. You respect your interviewer's time as much as your own.

At the close of the interview, you rise, shake hands, and thank the interviewer for his time. You smile. You tell him you enjoyed the interview and mention some facet of the conversation that was noteworthy—if there was such a moment. You don't make something up, since you know that people easily pick up on that kind of insincerity.

As you get ready to leave, you ask about the company's timetable for making a decision. After another expression of thanks, you're out the door.

After the Interview

The interview may be over, but it's not yet time to let your feelings show. The interview may have been wonderful, but it's best to contain your glee until you are well away from company premises. Keep a friendly and professional demeanor throughout.

The icing on the cake of the ideal interview is the perfect thank-you letter. It should thank the interviewer for taking the time to meet with you. After such a good interview, there is no need to make up for some weak point in the conversation, but the note can mention a topic that was raised. If you have something new to say, keep it brief and don't make it too much of a sales pitch. Say that you are excited about the position, but avoid talking about the idea that you'd be perfect for the job.

Since the note's content is more important than its form, email will do the job. A better option, though, especially as a follow-up to the ideal interview, is a printed letter that reaches the interviewer through the mail. With email, one more message in an overflowing inbox is unlikely to get much attention or have much effect.

After the ideal interview, should you make phone calls to the company? The one acceptable call is the one you make at the end of the interviewer's estimated time for making a decision. Otherwise, there is nothing to do but wait. The worst option is to call repeatedly. Top candidates have lost jobs to runners-up by calling again and again. That's not the behavior that a hiring manager hopes to see in a colleague.

Regardless of the outcome, take heart. Perfection is not part of the real world, and the ideal interview may be forever out of reach. Aim high, but remember that subjective self-evaluations are not terribly reliable. People have been hired after bad interviews. People have aced the interview and never heard another word. All you can do, through preparation and practice, is put yourself in the best possible position to be perfect.

The ancient aphorist, Publilius Syrus, said, "No one reaches a high position without daring," and the statement is as true today as it was in the corrupt Roman Empire he lived in. The daring he spoke of requires courage, but mainly against negative emotions within. You simply have to aim high, prepare thoroughly, and be willing to risk failure. The rewards are enormous, far greater than in his time, and you can achieve them.

If perfection will always be at least slightly out of reach, remember there is one very simple way to define the ideal interview: It's the one that got you the job.

References

Chapter 6: (Don't) Tell Me About Your Weaknesses

1. Newspaper advertisement, quoted in Steven Zohn, "Naïve Questions and Laughable Answers: An Eighteenth-Century Job Interview," in *Coll'astuzia, col giudizio: Essays in Honor of Neal Zaslaw*, ed. Cliff Eisen (Ann, Arbor, MI: Steglein, 2009), 62–92.

2. Steven Zohn, "Naïve Questions and Laughable Answers: An Eighteenth-Century Job Interview," in *Coll'astuzia, col giudizio: Essays in Honor of Neal Zaslaw*, ed. Cliff Eisen (Ann, Arbor, MI: Steglein, 2009), 62–92.

3. Friedrich Hurlebusch, quoted in Steven Zohn, "Naïve Questions and Laughable Answers: An Eighteenth-Century Job Interview," in *Coll'astuzia, col giudizio: Essays in Honor of Neal Zaslaw*, ed. Cliff Eisen (Ann, Arbor, MI: Steglein, 2009), 62–92.

Chapter 11: The New Interview, Courtesy of Google and Others

1. Allen I. Huffcutt and Winfred Arthur Jr, "Hunter and Hunter (1984) Revisited: Interview Validity for Entry-Level Jobs," *Journal of Applied Psychology* 79, no. 2 (1994): 184–90.

2. John C. Flanagan, "The Critical Incident Technique," *Psychological Bulletin* 51, no. 4 (1954): 327–58.

3. Ibid.

4. Karen Freeman, "John Flanagan, 90, Psychologist Who Devised Pilot Aptitude Test," *New York Times*, April 28, 1996.

5. William Poundstone, *Are You Smart Enough to Work at Google?* (New York: Little, Brown and Company, 2012).

6. Ken Auletta, *Googled: The End of the World as We Know It* (New York: Penguin Press, 2009), 98.

Chapter 13: A Guide to Salary Negotiation

1. Amy Gallo, "How to Negotiate Your Next Salary," *Harvard Business Review*, April 6, 2012.

Acknowledgments

I owe a huge debt to the people who have hired me, employed me, and mentored me at the jobs I've held. They enabled my professional hoboism, which gave me sufficient expertise to help others improve their careers and to write this book. This is only a partial list, with apologies for omissions:

Leo Lee and Susan Horwitz trained me in radio production and connected me to NPR, which actually aired my stories. John Fang hired me as an editor at *Asian Week*, which Herb Caen called "affirmative action in reverse," perhaps after reading my review of Henry's Hunan Restaurant. Maggie Canon hired me as a senior editor at *InfoWorld*, which really started the big career. Will Hearst allowed me to cover Silicon Valley at the *San Francisco Examiner*. When I wanted to do more than write about high tech, David Liddle saw the potential for yet another career transition and hired me to join Interval Research. My friend and colleague Bonnie Johnson connected me to McKinsey &

Company, which initiated something new, again. I appreciate all of them for the opportunities.

Thanks also to friends and associates who linked me to sources, documents, ideas, and contacts over the years. Dan McNeill has been a great friend and colleague with astute observations on so many topics, and Howard Bailen, the best friend of all, who found needles in haystacks and on websites, and always offered support. I've also benefited from the career-counseling expertise of Michelle Penn Swanson, Amy Pedersen, Dan Dorotik, and Gayle Keefer. Deborah Wallis provided insights that were always helpful.

The manuscript benefited from the copyediting and patience of Vanessa Mickan, whose enthusiasm for the project revived me during the home stretch.

Thanks, also, to Amy Collins, Bethany Brown, and Michele DeFilippo for their guidance on a new trail. And to Jason Garvey, who has contributed enormous web design and business support and friendship.

As always, my appreciation and love to Jeannie, Edan, and Max.

About Paul Freiberger

Paul Freiberger is the author or coauthor of five books, including *Fire in the Valley: The Making of the Personal Computer* (with Michael Swaine) and *Fuzzy Logic* (with Daniel McNeill). *Fire in the Valley* was made into the movie *Pirates of Silicon Valley*, which was nominated for five Emmy Awards. *Fuzzy Logic* won the *Los Angeles Times* Book Award. Freiberger provides career improvement services at his firm Shimmering Resumes. He has a BA in history from the State University of New York at Binghamton and a Masters in Italian from Middlebury College.

Index

"about me" interview question
  answer directed toward audience, 56–60
  common mistakes in answering, 61–2
  importance of, 50–3
  talking to resume and, 54–6, 58–9
accents, foreign, 189–90
acronyms
  industry, 12
  military, 188
age
  discrimination based on, 195–6
  illegal questions about, 100
agrarian societies, "jobs" in, 41–2
A.M. Best, 16
ambush interviews, 37–8

Americans with Disabilities act, 191
"anchoring effect," 180–2
appearance, job seeker's, 39, 196–8, 206–8
Astaire, Fred, 201
Auletta, Ken, 148
Aviation Psychogy Program, USAAF's, 137

Baroque era, job interviews in, 70–5
behavioral interview approach, 88–92, 131–2, 137–9
Better Business Bureau, 16
body language, 207–8
Brin, Sergey, 148
Buffett, Warren, 4
Bureau of Labor Statistics, website of, 8
Business Journals, The, 15

character, 3–4
Clemans, William, 138
clothing, appropriate, 39, 196–8, 206
coding exercises, Google's, 134–6
company research, 3, 13–17, 86, 92, 205–6
competence, core, 3–4, 54, 57–9, 131. *See also* skill sets.
confidence, 3
Cornell University Career Services, 22
"creative" interview questions, 52, 120, 136, 141–6
  Edison's, 127–30
  See also Google, problem-solving interview questions *and* "trick" questions.
credibility, establishing, 77
criminal history, illegal questions about, 101–2
critical incident technique (CIT), 137–9

degrees, 9
design-based interview questions, 145–6
desired salary, 172–7
disabilities
  American with Disabilities Act and, 191

discrimination based on, 101, 191–2
illegal questions about, 101, 191–2
interviewees with, 190–2
discrimination
age and, 100, 195–6
criminal history and, 101–2
disabilities and, 101, 191–2
family status and, 101
illegal interview questions and, 98–109
marital status and, 101
place of birth and, 100
race and, 99–100
religion and, 100
sexual orientation and, 100–1

EDGAR site, 15
Edison, Thomas, 127–30, 137
Ericksen, S.C., 138
etiquette
informational interviews and, 31–2
interview, 207
thank-you letters and, 31, 93, 95, 123–6

Facebook, networking and, 23
false job postings, 200
family status, illegal questions about, 101

federal law, interview
  questions and, 97–8
firing, history of, 193–4
fit, job, 3–4, 163
Flanagan, John C., 137–9
follow-through,
    post-interview
  importance of, 123–6
  informational interviews
    and, 31–2
  panel interviews and, 93,
    95–6
  phone calls and, 214
  thank-you letters and, 31,
    93, 95, 123–6, 213–14

Galinsky, Adam, 181–2
Google, interview style of,
    52, 120, 133–6, 133–6,
    140–8
group interviews. *See* panel
    interviews.

headhunters, questions to
    ask, 154–6
HR personnel
  compliance with
    regulations and, 108
  questions to ask, 156–8
  salary negotiation and,
    183–4
  screening by, 112
hiring managers
  illegal questions asked by,
    98

questions to ask, 158–60
Hurlebusch, Conrad
    Friedrich, 73–4

image, job seeker's, 204–8
Industrial Revolution, nature
    of jobs and, 41–2, 126–7
industry research, 8, 11–13,
    25, 205–6
informational interviews
  basics of, 20–1
  benefits of, 21–2, 32–3
  day of, 29–30
  etiquette for, 31–2
  follow-through for, 31–2
  networking and, 20, 22–5,
    32
  obtaining, 25–6
  opportunities for, 22–5
  protocols for, 30–1
  questions for, 26–9
internal hiring, 199–200
Internet, networking and,
    22–5
internships, 10
interpersonal skills, 3–4
"interview," defined, 10
interview-/job-performance
    correlation, 132–3

jargon
  industry, 12
  military, 188
job changes, frequent, 192–3
"job," defined, 10

job descriptions, 55–7
job interviews
   in Baroque era, 70–5
   in modern era, 126–30
   introduction of structured,
     137–41
jobs, history of, 40–3
job success, drive for, 4

Lee, Alissa, 148
legality of interview
   questions, 97–8
   discrimination and,
     98–102, 196
   indirect questions and, 98,
     102–3
   responding to illegal
     questions and, 102–8
lingo. *See* jargon.
LinkedIn, 23–5
local law, interview
   questions and, 97
long-time employment, one
   company, 194–5

Mamet, David, 60
marital status, illegal
   questions about, 101
mathematics-related
   interview questions,
     142–3
McGinn, Kathleen, 184
McKinsey & Company, x–xi
Michelangelo, 74–5
Microsoft, interview style of,
   52, 120, 142

military service, 188–9
mock interviews, 5

Neolithic Revolution, "jobs"
   during, 40–1
nepotism, 200
networking
   informational interviews
     and, 20, 22–5, 32
   online, 22–5
nonmonetary compensation,
   177, 182, 185
non-native English speakers,
   189–90

online networking, 22–5
overqualification, 195

Page, Larry, 148
panel interviews, 83
   behavioral questions
     during, 88–92
   follow-through for, 93, 95–6
   phone interviews and, 37
   preparation for, 86–8
   protocol for, 93–5
   purpose of, 84–5
   questions for panel in, 92,
     94
   research for, 85–6
   situational questions
     during, 88–92
personality, 3
phone interviews
   ambush interviews and,
     37–8

basics of, 38–9
conduct during, 46–8
group (panel) interviews
and, 37
image projected during,
39–40
increasing use of, 35–6
preparation for, 43–6
resumes and, 44–5
screening and, 36–7
place of birth, illegal
questions about, 100
prestige, company's, 14
problem-solving questions,
51–2, 120. *See also*
"creative" interview
questions *and* Google.
psychological interviews,
132
Public Register, The, 15

qualifications. *See*
competence, core *and*
skill sets.
questions, interview
"about me" question and,
50–62
behavioral, 88–92, 131–2,
137–9
"creative," 52, 120, 127–30,
136, 141–6
Edison's, 127–30, 137
Google's, 52, 120, 133–6,
133–6, 140–8
illegal. *See* legality of
interview questions.

reasons for wanting the
job and, 208–11
resumes and, 54–6
situational, 88–92, 137–9
small companies vs. large
companies and, 108–9
technology-related, 51–3,
120, 134–5
"trick" questions and,
111–21
weaknesses and, 63–82
questions, to interviewers
effective, 212–13
importance of, 150–2
kinds of, 152–64
rules of thumb when
asking, 164–6
salary-related, 170–1

race, illegal questions about,
99–100
Raphael, 74
recruiters, questions for,
154–6
rehearsal, 4–6, 59–60, 91–2,
206
rejection, handling, 198–201
religion, illegal questions
about, 100
relocation, 14
research
company, 3, 13–17, 86, 92,
205–6
importance of, 2–3, 7–8
industry, 8, 11–13, 25,
205–6

research (*cont.*)
  informational interviews
    and, 19
  job responsibilities and,
    55–7
  panel interviews and,
    85–6
  salary negotiations and,
    169–70
resumes
  alternatives to, 89
  frequent job changes and,
    192
  interview questions about,
    54–6
  online networking and,
    23–4
  phone interviews and,
    44–5
  resume writers and, 192
  "talking to," 54–6, 58–9,
    61–2
  targeted, 13
  weak points in, 5
Riley Guide, The, 15

salary and compensation
  answering questions
    about, 117–18, 172
  ranges in, 173–5, 179–83
  See also nonmonetary
    compensation *and*
    salary negotiations.
salary negotiations
  asking about salary and,
    170–1

desired salary and, 172–7
determining one's worth
  and, 168–70
expectations about, 177
leverage in, 171–2
researching to prepare for,
  169–70
salary history and, 172–7
strategies for, 177–85
See also salary and
  compensation.
screeners, employment, 36–7,
  173–5
Securities and Exchange
  Commission, 15
sexual orientation, illegal
  questions about, 100–1
situational interview
  questions, 88–92, 137–9
skill sets
  industry trends and, 8
  mapping to company
    needs, 54–9, 151–2,
    161–2
  updating, 8–10
  See also competence, core.
Small Business
  Administration, U.S., 13
social networks, networking
  with, 23–5
state law, interview
  questions and, 97
story-based interview
  questions, 143–5
structured interviews, 88–92,
  132, 137–41

T. Rowe Price, 167
"talking to" resume, 54–6,
    58–9, 61–2
targeted resumes, 13
technology field, interview
    questions in, 51–3, 120,
    134–5
Telemann, Georg Philipp,
    73–4
terminations, job, 193–4
thank-you notes
    importance of, 123–6
    informational interviews
        and, 31
    panel interviews and, 93,
        95
    post-interview follow-
        through, 31, 93, 95,
        123–6, 213–14
titles, military, 188–9
"trick" questions, 111–21

unique selling propositions,
    job seekers', 61–2

veterans, 188–9

weaknesses, questions about
    addressing in panel
        interviews, 87
    as "trap," 65–6
    credibility and, 77–8
    ineffective answers to,
        66–7, 80–1
    obvious weaknesses and,
        78–80
    one of big three questions,
        63–4
    purpose of, 67–9, 81–2
    turning into strengths,
        69–70, 75–7, 81, 211

Yahoo! Finance, 15

Zohn, Steven, 73–4

For Bulk Orders

For bulk orders of *When Can You Start?*
contact: Career Upshift Productions

Email: Info@careerupshiftproductions.com
Phone: 877-796-9737